The Open University

Business School

Unit 1

The purpose and context of financial accounting and reporting

Written by Jane Frecknall-Hughes

Module Team

Dr Devendra Kodwani, *B291 Chair & Author*

Dr Carien van Mourik, *Author*

Professor Jane Frecknall-Hughes, *Professional Certificate in Accounting Chair & Author*

Catherine Gowthorpe, *Author*

Kelly Dobbs, *Curriculum Assistant*

Elizabeth R Porter, *Regional Manager*

Sam Cooper, *Programme Coordinator*

Emir Forken, *Qualifications Manager*

Dr Lesley Messer, *Programme Manager*

Funmi Mapelujo, *Curriculum Manager*

External Assessor

Professor Stuart Turley, Manchester Business School

Critical Readers

Professor Judy Day, Manchester Business School

Elizabeth R Porter

Professor Peter Walton

Developmental Testers

Dr Teodora Burnand

Sam Cooper

Vimal Goricha

Vani Shri Goswami

Dudley Hughes

Production Team

Martin Brazier, *Graphic Designer*

Anne Brown, *Media Assistant*

Sarah Cross, *Print Buyer*

Beccy Dresden, *Media Project Manager*

Vicky Eves, *Graphic Artist*

Paul Hoffman, *Editor*

Diane Hopwood, *Rights Assistant*

Kelvin Street, *Library*

Software

Accounting package software was designed by and remains the property of Sage plc.

Other Material

The Module Team wishes to acknowledge use of some material from B680 *The Certificate in Accounting*.

This publication forms part of the Open University module B291 *Financial accounting*. Details of this and other Open University modules can be obtained from the Student Registration and Enquiry Service, The Open University, PO Box 197, Milton Keynes MK7 6BJ, United Kingdom (tel. +44 (0)845 300 60 90; email general-enquiries@open.ac.uk).

Alternatively, you may visit the Open University website at www.open.ac.uk where you can learn more about the wide range of modules and packs offered at all levels by The Open University.

To purchase a selection of Open University materials visit www.ouw.co.uk, or contact Open University Worldwide, Walton Hall, Milton Keynes MK7 6AA, United Kingdom for a brochure (tel. +44 (0)1908 858793; fax +44 (0)1908 858787; email ouw-customer-services@open.ac.uk).

The Open University

Walton Hall

Milton Keynes

MK7 6AA

First published 2010. Second edition 2012.

Edited and designed by The Open University.

Typeset in India by OKS Prepress Services, Chennai.

Printed in the Great Britain by Henry Ling Limited, at the Dorset Press, Dorchester, DT1 1HD

ISBN 978 1 7800 7353 8

2.1

Contents

Introduction

Welcome to the first unit of B291 *Financial accounting*.

Unit 1 serves as an introduction to B291. It establishes the framework within which accounting now resides and presents a view of likely future developments. It sets the context for the remaining units in the module and, given its introductory nature, you will find that it covers many concepts quite quickly and briefly. This does not mean that they are unimportant. You will be returning to them in more detail in later units, so make sure that you understand thoroughly the material in this unit before going on to the rest of the module.

Unit 1 consists of four sessions.

Session 1 introduces the basic terminology, purpose and different types of accounting.

Session 2 details the organisational context of financial accounting and what accounting information is used for and by whom.

Session 3 tells you about the environmental influences and constraints on business and accounting and introduces regulatory frameworks and structures.

Session 4 discusses the conceptual frameworks, concepts and principles underlying accounting and financial reporting information.

By the end of Unit 1, you should have a clear understanding of how accountants act as processors and purveyors of information for decision making, of the needs of those who use accounting information, and of the role performed by accountants as well as being aware of relevant regulatory and conceptual frameworks. Accounting does not exist for its own sake or in a vacuum: there must be a reason why accounting is being done. Unit 1 should also enable you to understand the relevance of the remainder of the module to your own career, if you are thinking about becoming a professionally qualified accountant.

Learning aims and outcomes of Unit 1

Upon completion of Unit 1 you are expected to be able to understand and explain:

1   the purposes of bookkeeping and accounting
2   the context in which accounting information fulfils its various functions
3   the main environmental influences and constraints on business and accounting
4   conceptual frameworks, such as the International Accounting Standards Board (IASB) *Conceptual Framework for Financial Reporting* and the Accounting Standards Board (ASB) *Statement of Principles for Financial Reporting*, the qualitative characteristics of accounting information and the concepts and principles of accounting.

SESSION **1 The purpose of accounting**

Introduction

Upon completion of Session 1 you are expected to be able to:
- define bookkeeping and accounting
- explain the general purposes and functions of accounting
- explain the differences between management and financial accounting
- describe the main elements of financial accounting information – assets, liabilities, revenue and expenses
- identify the main financial statements and their purposes.

In Session 1 you will learn about what accounting is, the purposes for which accounting information is used, how to distinguish between management and financial accounting, the components of accounting information, and the main financial reports in which this information is presented to its users.

1.1 Definitions of bookkeeping, accounting and reporting

First of all, you need to be aware of some of the basic terminology in this subject area. There are several different terms in common use under the general umbrella of accounting and they are often used by people interchangeably without distinguishing the meanings of these terms. Some of the most important are considered below, namely bookkeeping, accounting and reporting.

1.1.1 Bookkeeping

Bookkeeping is the process of recording transactions in the financial records of a business entity. Unit 2 looks in more detail at what a transaction is, but for now we shall consider it as any sort of occurrence that has a financial effect. Before transactions are recorded, they need to be classified according to their type so that similar items can be recorded in the same record or account. For example, a business entity will keep records of sales and purchases of goods or services, each classified according to their nature. Originally records detailing similar types of transactions were kept together in a book or ledger, with one or more pages dedicated to a particular kind of transaction, for example, sales of specific goods. Therefore, records often are collectively referred to as the 'books' of a business.

Bookkeeping goes back many hundreds, even thousands, of years. It began because people needed to record business transactions as a means of keeping track of who owed them money and to whom they owed money, and of knowing whether businesses were financially successful or not. For many years, bookkeeping was based on common sense – businesses recorded the data they considered necessary in order to obtain the information they required. 'Bookkeeping' as a term is used to denote not only recording transactions in the way described here, but also frequently as an abbreviation for double-entry bookkeeping, a particular system of recording transactions devised about 500 years ago, and first written about by an Italian monk called Luca Pacioli. Today, double-entry bookkeeping remains the most widespread method of bookkeeping and it will be discussed further in Units 2 and 3 of this module.

Portrait of Luca Pacioli
(c.1445–c.1514)
Mathematician and Friend
of Leonardo da Vinci, 1495
by Jacopo de'Barbari
(1440/50–a.1515) Museo e
Gallerie Nazionale di
Capodimonte, Naples,
Italy/Bridgeman Art
Library.

Portrait of Luca Pacioli

It is the job of the bookkeeper to maintain the books of a business and keep them up to date. This is done by ensuring that transactions are recorded in a timely and logical manner, either chronologically, as they occur, or by dealing with like items in batches, for example, recording all sales of a particular good in a defined period of time (day, week or month, according to the needs of a business). Recording may be done manually using paper and pen, but it is now more commonly done by using a computerised bookkeeping or accounting program.

Recording items in individual accounts (see above) is also referred to as posting, and a computer program can ensure that all necessary records are completed quickly and accurately (provided that data have been entered correctly, of course!).

Link between accounting and writing

Arguably the need felt by the Sumerian civilisation in Mesopotamia to keep account of livestock was also the origin of writing, as this account was recorded. The concept of 'wealth' is much older than that of 'money'. Livestock was often regarded as an indication of wealth – which is still the case in some developing countries. Anyone who has read Alexander McCall Smith's *The No. 1 Ladies' Detective Agency*, set in Botswana in recent years, will recall that Mma Ramotse was bequeathed a herd of 180 prime cattle by her father, who had regarded them as an investment.

As a result of posting transaction details to individual accounts in this way, each account will show a history or list of transactions that have occurred, so the management of a business can keep track of them individually. It can also track movements (increases and decreases in the volume of transactions recorded) over a period of time (e.g., to monitor sales of a new product). Businesses also need to know how well they are faring in all aspects, and the existence of accounts enables them to draw up a formal report to show this. The list of monetary transactions in an individual account can be totalled so, for example, the total sales of a good in a particular period can be determined. This totalling of individual accounts also may reveal that one side of a double-entry account exceeds another in value. This enables a balance to be calculated. The individual account balances for all accounts are then listed in a separate document, which is known as a trial balance. The process of balancing off individual accounts and drawing up a trial balance is an important part of determining whether a business has made a profit or loss overall. This process will be covered in Units 2 and 3 of this module.

Activity 1.1 ....

(Note: you should never look at the answer that follows before attempting an activity.)

Imagine a business recorded what it had sold, to whom, the date it was sold, the price at which it was sold, and the date it received payment from the customer, along with similar data concerning the purchases made by the business.

What information do you think that the business could produce from these data? Take ten minutes or so to write down your answer.

Feedback ....

These data would enable the business to know how much it had sold and how much it had purchased, how much cash it had received and paid, how much was owing to it and how much was owed by it (both in respect of any individual customer or supplier and in respect of the overall business transactions), and whether it was making a profit or a loss over a particular time period. It might also be possible to compare how much had been sold to the customer and purchased from the supplier with amounts sold and purchased previously.

1.1.2 Accounting and reporting

Accounting is a process which identifies, organises, classifies, records, summarises and communicates information about economic events, usually, but not exclusively, in monetary terms. While accounting is often considered as including bookkeeping as well, it is much wider than bookkeeping. It may also be regarded as a transformative process in that it turns the raw data recorded in bookkeeping into useful information. Data lack meaning until they have been processed into meaningful information. What good is it to know that a book cost a bookshop £10? Those data will only become information when they are combined with something else that enables you to assess them within a relevant context, such as how much the book would have cost had the bookshop bought it from a different supplier or how much profit the bookshop made when it sold the book to a customer.

The communication aspect of accounting involves the reporting of information about a business to interested parties, such as owners and managers. Results of all transactions over a period of time need to be summarised, presented and interpreted in order to assess a business's performance and its financial position at a given date. The period of time for which results are calculated is referred to as an accounting period or period of account. An accounting period can be any length of time, and the length may be determined by the reason for which a set of results is required, for example, to provide management with information, to support an application for a bank loan, etc. Commonly, however, an accounting period is of a year's duration, and however often businesses produce sets of results, they will always produce an annual set of results, as these are required for specific purposes, such as for taxation or, in the case of companies, filing with a regulatory authority. Only in certain well defined circumstances will sets of results for periods other than a year be accepted for these specific purposes. For example, the first accounting period for companies in the UK must be more than six months, but no more than 18 months.

The date on which an annual accounting period ends is referred to as the business's accounting reference date or closing date. For UK business entities, this date can be any date in the year and does not have to coincide with a calendar year, though this is not necessarily the case elsewhere. The form in which results are presented is usually twofold: a calculation of the business's overall profit or loss for its accounting period, referred to as an income statement or profit and loss statement/account; and a statement of financial position as at the end of the accounting period, also called a balance sheet. In this module we will use the terms 'income statement' and 'balance sheet'. The income statement and balance sheet together are often referred to as the financial statements or set of accounts.

Different accounting terminology

The different names for the different parts of financial statements have arisen as a result of different customs, rules and regulations over the years, which are considered in more detail later in this unit, when we look especially at the impact of the International Accounting Standards Board (IASB) and the introduction of International Accounting Standards (IASs) and International Financial Reporting Standards (IFRSs). 'Profit and loss account' was for many years a common term, but it was felt to be less than precise, particularly when, for example, it was used by entities which did not have a profit motive, such as charities. IAS 1, the international accounting standard which deals with the presentation of financial statements, therefore, introduced the term 'income statement', which can be more universally applied. At the same time, it suggested the replacement of another, much older term, 'balance sheet', by the term 'statement of financial position'. IAS 1, however, did not make adoption of the new terms mandatory. 'Income statement' has been widely adopted, but not 'statement of financial position'. While many professional accounting training manuals use the latter, it is not yet widely used by businesses, which still continue to use the term 'balance sheet'. In this module, we therefore use the terms 'income statement' and 'balance sheet'. In addition to widespread use, the term 'balance sheet' is also useful when learning accounting as it helps remind you that a balance sheet itself should 'balance', that is, both halves/sides should add up to the same figure, and that certain individual account balances will be included there. You will learn more about this when you get to grips with the mechanics of double-entry bookkeeping in Units 2 and 3 of this module.

Although businesses produce formal income statements and balance sheets for, and at the end of, accounting periods, they can do so at any time, and often produce them more regularly to help managers monitor and control business activities and make decisions, as mentioned above. This adds further dimensions to accounting, as it helps look to the future, rather than focusing on transactions that have already occurred, and in this sense accounting has a management function, as a part or sub-set of the wider management information system (MIS) of a business. In this context, accounting is sometimes referred to as an accounting information system (AIS) or in short, accounting system.

Activity 1.2   ....

Earlier it was mentioned that it might not be very useful to know only that a book cost a bookshop £10. What other data do you think could be used in order to convert the data about the cost of the book into information? Take ten minutes or so to think about this and write down your answer.

Feedback   ....

You may have suggested any of the following:

● the selling price of the book

● the amount the bookshop could have purchased the book for elsewhere

● the time it took to receive the book from the publisher after the bookshop ordered it

● the condition of the book when it arrived in the bookshop

● the length of time before payment was effected.

These are all good answers, and there are probably many others. In each case, they provide the means of assessing something:

● the profit that will be made if the book is sold

● whether the bookshop paid a 'good' price for the book

● how far in advance the bookshop should order the book if it wants it to be available for customers on a particular date

● whether the supplier packages books appropriately

● possibly, whether the business is likely to be given credit by the supplier in future.

Information is data processed for a purpose. Once data have been converted into information, you can then use that information to help you make a decision, which will require the exercise of judgement. You cannot take meaningful decisions with data. This process can be expressed as follows:

Decision = Purpose + Information + Judgement

Note that while the bookkeeper will record data, it is the accountant who (as the definition of 'accounting' suggests) will convert data into information which serves a purpose, that is, is useful. To be useful, information must be timely, relevant, complete and of good quality. It can only possess these qualities if the underlying data have been recorded properly.

1.2 Reasons for and objectives of accounting

The main purpose of accounting is to provide financial information to managers and owners of businesses (as we have already seen) and a variety of other interested parties (as you will learn in Session 2). This financial information fulfils different objectives, namely stewardship, accountability, planning and decision making and control, as discussed below.

1.2.1   Stewardship

Persons who run or manage businesses are not always those who have invested money and/or resources in the business. They manage money and/or resources which are owned by others, and act as stewards (or agents) on behalf of owners (sometimes called principals). The concept of stewardship places an obligation on stewards to provide financial information relating to the resources which they control, but do not own (see Figure 1 below).

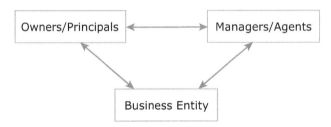

Figure 1 Stewardship

1.2.2   Accountability

Accountability is connected to the idea of stewardship (though it is a wider concept as it may extend to other stakeholders or society in general). Stewards are obliged to give to owners of businesses an account of how they have managed resources. This may be discharged in part by the provision of financial information, such as an income statement and balance sheet. However, the idea of 'accountability' also carries with it the notion of acting responsibly and being able to justify one's actions and, therefore, prepared to suffer the consequences of irresponsible and unjustifiable actions. The issues relating to accountability will be discussed in detail in Unit 6.

1.2.3   Planning and decision making

Business managers need to have financial information to enable them to make plans for future business activities and operations. For example, if a business plans to sell 120,000 units of a good it manufactures in the next year, it will need to know the quantity and price of raw materials required to make 120,000 units, the number of staff required and the hours each staff member can work and their rate of pay, the type and number of machines required, etc. There will, of course, be other costs associated with production. Such information is typically derived from on-going business activities and experience and reported financial information, combined with knowledge of future price increases for raw materials, wages and other known costs. Planning of this kind can be very difficult in practice if a business is aiming to increase or decrease production of an existing good, and becomes even more difficult in the case of producing any good which the business has not produced before.

1.2.4 Control

Accounting information can also be used for the purposes of control. Business managers need to monitor activities and operations to see whether they are proceeding according to plan. In the example in Section 1.2.3 of planning to manufacture and sell 120,000 units of a good, a business may have planned to sell the units evenly over a year, that is, 10,000 units per calendar month. Therefore, the business will need accounting information on a monthly basis to see whether this target is being achieved. If it is not, then the business will need to find out why, and take corrective action if possible. The type of corrective action will depend on the problem that has been identified. Different problems can have the same overall effect. For example, if sales were 'down' in any given month, it might be the case that trade was more seasonal than anticipated and there might be compensating higher sales in other months. It might also have been the case that a sales representative for a particular area had been away on sick leave, which would also result in lower sales. Equally, a production problem could have prevented sufficient goods being manufactured for sale – perhaps being caused by machines breaking down or suppliers' inability to deliver raw materials when needed. It is also possible that sales in a given month might be 'up' on what was forecast – which could also cause problems if it continued in the longer term, as the business may have resources that are inadequate to meet an unanticipated higher demand. Regular provision of accounting information (in this example, for sales and production) is essential for control purposes.

Planning, decision making and control are aspects of accounting which will be covered in B292 *Management accounting*.

Activity 1.3

How do you think a shareholder in a company can be assured that the financial statements give a true and fair view of how the directors have been running the company? Take ten minutes or so to write down your answer.

Feedback

The shareholder would primarily look at the externally audited financial statements for the accounting period ended most recently. You might have been thinking along the lines of the shareholder asking someone to undertake an independent investigation into the financial statements and (by implication) into the directors' management activities. You would have been right, because this is what external auditing involves. An **external auditor** is an independent, external person or firm appointed formally by the shareholders to write a report to them on the externally reported financial results of a company (as shown in its financial statements) and on its management. You will learn more about the role of the auditor in Unit 6. There are also **internal auditors**, who might do a similar job, but report to internal committees within a firm. (See Section 2.4, which looks at shareholders as one of the key stakeholders who have an interest in financial statements.)

1.3 Management and financial accounting

From Section 1.2, it is clear that accounting information has a number of different purposes, governed by the needs of those using it. This brings us to consider different types of accounting, namely financial accounting and management accounting, as the purposes fulfilled by accounting information generally fall under one or the other heading. It is important to note that this does not mean that any different types of books or records need to be kept. It is just that the information produced from the books and records organises, classifies, summarises and communicates information according to the perspectives and needs of the users, as Table 1 below shows.

Table 1 Differences between financial and management accounting

	Financial accounting	*Management accounting*
Chief purpose	Production of summarised income statements and balance sheets by managers as a formal report on the stewardship of resources entrusted to them but should also, in the case of public companies (see Session 2), help interested parties (such as investors) make decisions. Depending on the type of the business entity, documents may be publicly available.	Production of detailed and up to date information used by managers to plan activities and control them. This information is not publicly available, but is internal to the entity producing it.
When information is prepared	Annually, at the end of an accounting period, but, depending on the type of business entity, may be every three or six months as well.	Normally prepared on a monthly basis.
Governed by	Legal requirements and often mandatory accounting regulations* and/ or conventions which may also dictate a required format (though this depends on the legal form of an entity).	Management needs only – with no legal requirement to produce anything in any format, or anything at all. Information is produced in the format management deems most useful, e.g., by operating unit or product line, to record and monitor sales (by product, region, etc.), costs of production methods or products.
Perspective	Gives information about past performance, and might in practice be outdated by the time summarised documents are produced.	Comparative and up to date. While a given month's results are provided, these are usually accompanied by a total for all months to date and comparative figures for a prior year (as well as for planned activities in the month and period to date).

* In order to facilitate comparison between similar business entities, income statements, balance sheets and other summarised accounting documents are prepared using accepted conventions and standards. This is covered in Session 4.

B291 focuses on financial accounting, while management accounting forms the focus of B292.

Activity 1.4

Which of the following statements is untrue?

1 Financial statements are usually produced annually and management accounts are usually produced monthly.

2 Financial statements are more accurate than management accounts.

3 Financial statements may be audited by an external auditor and management accounts are not audited.

4 Financial statements are intended primarily for external users and management accounts for internal purposes.

Take ten minutes or so to write down your answer.

Feedback

All statements are true, though in the case of Statement 2, it does depend on the extent to which financial or management accounts may contain estimated figures, which are appropriate in certain circumstances, as you will learn later. Remember that all accounting information is produced from the same records – but at different times and for different purposes. It should all be of similar quality. Note that, in respect of Statement 3, while management accounts are not audited, not all financial statements are either, hence the subtle use of the phrase 'may be audited' in respect of financial statements. The requirement for audit is determined by the type of organisation and its size. Again, you will learn more about this in Unit 6.

1.4 The main elements of accounting information

Section 1.1.2 told you that results of all business transactions over a period of time need to be summarised, presented and interpreted in order to assess a business's performance and its financial position at a given date, in the form of an income statement and balance sheet. It was emphasised in Section 1.3 that the presentation of financial accounting information is governed by a combination of legal requirements and accounting regulations and conventions. Different types of business entities are governed by different requirements, and this is dealt with in Session 2. However, one of the rationales underlying the preparation of income statements and balance sheets is to turn raw financial data into useful information, and this is achieved in part by organising, classifying and presenting data in particular ways to make them meaningful. Here we shall look at some conventional ways of doing this.

1.4.1 Income and expenses

An income statement is a summarised financial statement which shows how well or badly a business is faring. An example of an income statement is shown in Figure 2. This is an income statement for a hypothetical sole trader (here called Mr Schmidt), a type of business entity you will learn about later in Session 2.

Mr Schmidt
Income statement for the year ended 31 March 2010

	£	£
Sales		40,000
Less: Cost of goods sold		
Opening inventory	14,000	
Purchases	22,000	
	36,000	
Less: Closing inventory	(12,000)	
		(24,000)
Gross profit		16,000
Less: Expenses		
Rent	3,000	
Lighting and heating expenses	2,800	
General expenses	800	
		(6,600)
Net profit		9,400

Figure 2   Example of an income statement

As its name suggests, an 'income statement' includes all the income generated by a business in its accounting period. This is usually derived from the sales of its products and services, which are first listed from individual accounts on to the trial balance and then added up together. Income derived from sales may be referred to by a number of different terms, such as turnover or sales (sometimes sales turnover), sales revenue or just revenue. However, income may be derived from other sources, and the source may be denoted in the terminology used to describe it. If a business derives income from a bank account in the form of bank interest, for example, this too will be included in the income statement. It will be shown separately from income arising from sales and will be called 'bank interest receivable' or something similar. However, perhaps rather unhelpfully for persons learning about accounting for the first time, 'revenue' can also be used as a general term to mean any sort of income, and if so used, could include 'bank interest' as well. There is no hard and fast rule about how the terms 'income' or 'revenue' are used. They are both very common terms, and you will see both used in this module.

In acquiring or making products for sale, or delivering services to customers, however, a business will have laid out some of its own resources (most commonly, money). For example, if a business makes a product, it will need to buy in raw materials, pay wages to employees making the product, and pay for electricity (for example) used in the manufacturing process. Likewise all such items are listed from individual accounts on to the trial balance and then added up together, with like items grouped together. For example, raw materials will be added together, as will energy items, wages, etc. The term costs or expenses is often used here to denote these types of items. Some accounting textbooks differentiate between these terms, but you will find them used interchangeably without distinction of meaning, and we do not differentiate between them in this module. Often terms used in accounting are also used in every day life with no reference to their financial meanings and this contributes to the overall lack of precision. For example, it is common to speak of someone 'paying the price' for something, such as committing a misdemeanour.

An income statement shows the total costs subtracted/deducted from total income. If there is an excess of total income over total costs, this is referred to as a profit (sometimes called a surplus, if the entity, like a charity, does not have a profit motive). If total costs exceed total income, then a loss or deficit (the latter is often used by non-profit-making entities) is said to arise – hence the alternative name for an income statement of 'profit and loss account'. By organising, classifying and presenting income and expenses in this way, the income statement makes them into meaningful information because by calculating a profit or loss it becomes possible to determine how well or poorly a business is performing.

You will see that Mr Schmidt has separated his costs into those that relate to items that he has sold and the rest, and it shows two different kinds of profit. You will learn all about this later in this module, so do not worry if there are things here that you do not understand. Note also that the accounting convention used here puts figures to be deducted in round brackets. This is widely used, especially in the UK, but you should be aware that not every country uses it.

1.4.2   Assets and liabilities

As the income statement groups together like items of income and deducts like items of costs to show a profit or loss for an accounting period, the balance sheet also groups together like items to show the financial position of an entity at the end of its accounting period. It is rather like a 'snapshot' of the entity at that moment in time. Determining a financial position is something that individual people frequently do as well, and involves sorting out what, as a person, you own and what is of value to you, often in terms of money and things like houses, cars, jewellery, furniture, etc. These types of things are called assets and the term means much the same in an accounting context as well. Determining a financial position also involves sorting out what, as a person, you might owe to other people – by way of things like mortgages, loans, credit card bills, unpaid bills for utilities, etc. These are called liabilities. If the value of your assets exceeds your liabilities, you could (in theory, at least) sell your assets, realise cash and settle your liabilities.

Assets and liabilities have been carefully defined by the International Accounting Standards Board (IASB) (see Session 4 for more on this). Assets are resources controlled by a business as a result of past events and from which future economic benefits are expected to flow to the business. They might be things the business owns, like machinery.

Businesses try to establish a financial position in a similar way at the end of an accounting period. They may have various assets, such as land and buildings, plant and machinery and vehicles, which they use to carry out business, manufacture goods and deliver them, and which they intend to keep for a long time. These are referred to as non-current assets or fixed assets. 'Fixed' here does not necessarily imply that assets are immovably fixed in one place (though many kinds of these assets often are); rather, it implies 'lasting'. Many non-current assets, such as land and buildings, plant and machinery and vehicles, etc., are also referred to as tangible assets in that they have a physical form and can be 'touched' (the basic meaning of the word 'tangible'). It follows that there are also intangible assets which are things that cannot be 'touched', such as patents, copyrights, trademarks, etc., though their existence may be confirmed by some kind of documentation. Businesses may also have items which they have bought to use in manufacturing, such as raw materials, but have not yet used. These will be used up in the course of manufacturing, and are often referred to as inventory or stock. They form one of another category of assets known as current assets, which either stay with a business entity for only a short time, or change over time. They perform a different role in the business from non-current assets. A business will not have exactly the same type or amount of raw materials in stock at the end of every accounting period, but will keep buying in materials as and when required, as it continues to manufacture and sell goods, so from one accounting period end to another, these items will not be the same. Businesses may also have stocks of finished items, which have not yet been sold, or stocks of items which are only partly finished (work in progress).

Other types of current assets are cash and amounts due from customers who have not paid for goods sold to them, referred to as trade receivables ('receivables' for short and sometimes also referred to as trade debtors).

Businesses also have liabilities in a similar way to individuals. They buy from suppliers, and may not pay for goods immediately, so at the end of an accounting period may owe money for such goods, referred to as trade payables ('payables' for short and also sometimes referred to as trade creditors) or for utilities such as gas, electricity or telephone charges. Businesses also borrow money from banks or other lenders to start or continue business. Also, owners of businesses invest their own money in business, most often when business commences. Money, resources or assets put into a business by owners are referred to as owner's interest, equity or, commonly, as capital, though this latter word can be used to mean other things as well. As money, resources and assets will eventually be repayable to a business's owners, this may also be regarded as a type of liability. Generally, liability items are classified by reference to when they need to be paid. Those due more than a year after the end of the accounting period are referred to as non-current liabilities (or long-term liabilities). Those due within a year or less are called current liabilities. Amounts due in respect of trade payables will be current liabilities as such amounts are often due within three months or less, whereas loans may not be repayable for several years.

> Liabilities are present obligations of a business arising from past events, the settlement of which is expected to result in an outflow from the business of resources embodying economic benefits. They might be sums of money owed to lenders, for example, who have loaned money to a business, and who will need to be repaid in due course.

At the end of an accounting period, all assets and liabilities are listed from individual accounts on to the trial balance and then added up together, with like items grouped together. There are two ways of showing assets and liabilities on a balance sheet – using either a horizontal format or a vertical format. A horizontal format lists all the assets on the left-hand side and all the liabilities on the right. As a result of the manner in which transactions are recorded using double-entry bookkeeping (this is discussed further in Units 2 and 3), the total of assets always equals the total of liabilities. This is why a statement of financial position is commonly called a 'balance sheet', that is, both sides (or halves) add up to the same amount. A vertical format often shows capital in the 'bottom' half, and in the 'top' half shows assets with liabilities deducted from them (current liabilities, for example, are deducted from current assets to show net current assets or liabilities). This is often referred to as the net assets approach. It is also possible to show all assets in the top half and all liability (or credit) balances in the bottom half (which is now possible under the international accounting approach: different formats for financial statements will be covered in detail in Units 4 and 5). Any entity could, in theory, produce a balance sheet in either format, as it is just a matter of presentation. The vertical balance sheet (i.e., using the net assets approach) is common in the UK, but different countries have different rules. It would not, for example, be permitted in France, although other countries with specific regulations may require it for certain types of entities. Examples of a horizontal and vertical balance sheet are shown in Figures 3 and 4 below – again for Mr Schmidt, the hypothetical sole trader whose income statement you looked at previously, in Figure 2.

Mr Schmidt
Balance sheet as at 31 March 2010

	£		£
Non-current assets		Capital	
Fixtures and fittings	18,000	Cash introduced	25,000
		Retained earnings	11,000
Current assets		Net profit for the year	9,400
Inventory	12,000		
Trade receivables	5,800	Current liabilities	
Cash at bank and in hand	2,300	Trade payables	8,200
Drawings	15,500		
	53,600		53,600

Figure 3   Example of a horizontal balance sheet

Mr Schmidt
Balance sheet as at 31 March 2010

	£	£
Non-current assets		
Fixtures and fittings		18,000
Current assets		
Inventory	12,000	
Trade receivables	5,800	
Cash at bank and in hand	2,300	
	20,100	
Current liabilities		
Trade payables	(8,200)	
Net current assets		11,900
Net assets		29,900
Capital		
Cash introduced		25,000
Retained earnings		11,000
		36,000
Add: Net profit for the year		9,400
		45,400
Less: Drawings		(15,500)
		29,900

Figure 4   Example of a vertical balance sheet, following the net assets approach

Again, do not worry if there are things here that you do not understand, such as drawings or why these are included in the horizontal balance sheet with assets, as these will be explained later (though drawings are simply a withdrawal of capital by the owner(s)). You will see in the above balance sheets that both show the profit of £9,400, as per the income statement in Figure 2, included with the capital elements.

Activity 1.5 ....

Classify the following list of items as income, a cost/expense or an asset/liability:

1   a machine for manufacturing widgets
2   air conditioning used in a factory
3   sales of 1,000 widgets for cash to Mr Mohammad, a customer
4   £3,000 borrowed from the bank
5   a heap of metal on the yard, to be used for manufacturing widgets
6   £4,000 owed to Pyron Ltd for the metal in item 5
7   a Toyota Lexus car, used by an employee, but owned by his/her employer, Yen Ltd
8   £10,000 of personal savings used by someone starting up a business.

Take ten minutes or so to write down your answer.

Feedback ....

1   This is a tangible non-current asset – used for carrying out business and likely to be kept for a long time.
2   This is a cost/expense – utility needed to keep machinery and employees at an appropriate temperature while they work. If the actual air conditioning plant itself is implied by the words 'air conditioning' (rather than what the plant actually does) then this would be a tangible non-current asset, likely to be used and kept for a long time.
3   This is a sale to a customer, generating sales revenue (income).
4   This is a loan, which will have to be paid back. It is a liability, and whether it is classified as current or long-term will depend on the date of repayment.
5   This is raw material to be used in manufacturing so is inventory, hence it is a current asset.
6   This is money owed for material to be used in the business, so it represents a trade payable, and would be a current liability.
7   This is a non-current asset, as it is used in the business for transporting the employees (it may be what is called a 'pool' car, that is, it is available to a variety of employees). It is important to note that the car is owned by the employee's company, not the employee. Therefore, the car would be one of the company's non-current assets.
8   This is money introduced to do business – therefore, it is capital which may be regarded as a particular type of liability, in that it will eventually be repayable to the owner.

1.5 The main financial statements

To summarise from the previous discussions, the financial statements comprise:

- The income statement or profit and loss statement, which shows income, less costs/expenses for an accounting period. Where income exceeds expenses, a profit or surplus arises. Where costs/expenses exceed income, a loss or deficit arises.

- The balance sheet, which is a 'snapshot' of assets and liabilities at a moment in time – the end of the accounting period. The end of the accounting period is also often referred to as the 'accounting reference date', 'balance sheet date' or 'closing date'.

To the above, we must also add:

- The cash flow statement. There is a requirement for certain business entities, namely companies, to provide a cash flow statement to show movements in cash over the period covered by the income statement. This cash flow statement is considered by entities required to provide it as a third financial statement in addition to the income statement and balance sheet. The cash flow statement will be discussed later in this module when you learn about company financial statements, and examples will be given there.

If you look at any income statement and/or balance sheet for an entity, you will find that they are generally accompanied by a set of notes to the financial statements which provide further information, explanation or analyses, which are more conveniently shown separately from the main statements.

As you will come to learn in Session 4 and subsequent units of this module, 'profit' and 'cash' are not the same thing, although profit commonly becomes cash in time. It is important for a business to generate both – profit to stay in business in the longer term and cash to be able to pay bills and liabilities as they fall due.

Summary

This session has provided an introduction to some of the basics of accounting. You have learned the basic terminology of bookkeeping and accounting, the general purposes and functions of accounting and the differences between the two sorts of accounting (financial accounting and management accounting). You should also now be able to describe the different elements of financial information, such as income/revenue, costs/expenses, assets and liabilities, as well as identify the main financial statements (income statement, balance sheet and cash flow statement) and their purposes.

In Session 2 you will learn about the different organisational forms that exist for doing business and how accounting fulfils different functions in accordance with the primary goals of these organisations. Depending on their legal status, size, and whether they have shares which are sold on a stock exchange, business organisations have to follow more or less extensive accounting regulations and reporting requirements. Reporting regulations and requirements exist to protect the informational needs of a whole range of stakeholders.

SESSION **2 The context of accounting**

Introduction

Upon completion of Session 2 you are expected to be able to:

- identify and define different types of business entity and not-for-profit organisation – sole trader, partnership, private and public limited liability company, charity, governmental and non-governmental organisations
- explain the objectives of various business and other organisations
- identify and discuss the role of accounting in business and other organisations
- explain the functions of accounting in business organisations
- identify the main stakeholders in business and other organisations and discuss their information needs
- explain the need for recording transactions and the legal requirements for preparing financial statements for different organisations.

In Session 2 you will look at what the concept of 'business' means and the different objectives that business organisations may have. You will go on to learn about the different types of business organisation and will look at different ways of classifying them – by their primary activity, their legal form, by reference to their profit aims and to ownership or control. Different forms of business organisations are governed by different regulations, which affect the format in which they are required to present their financial statements. You will also learn about the functions of accounting in different types of organisation and the different types of entities and people who use and are interested in financial statements and why.

2.1 Business and its objectives

2.1.1 Defining business

The word business is often used very generally, and encompasses a variety of ideas. It can be used in the same way as other, rather general words, like firm or enterprise, simply to mean an entity designed to provide goods and/or services to consumers. It can also be used more widely to apply to a particular market sector, such as 'the car industry', or it can be very broad in meaning and encompass all activity undertaken by the whole community of suppliers of goods and services.

2.1.2 Business objectives

In capitalist economies, businesses are mostly privately owned and exist to earn profits for owners, though there is also a significant body of non-profit business in the form of non-government organisations (NGOs), charities, cooperatives and state owned enterprises, etc. Forms of business ownership vary, but there are several common forms, which will be considered in Section 2.2.

In socialist economies, business is generally owned and run by the state or state agencies. However, most, if not all, economies are mixed, that is, they contain both privately owned and state owned businesses, though there is no single definition for what 'mixed' means or implies, as economies as different as those of the USA and Cuba have been termed 'mixed'.

2.2 Classifying business organisations

2.2.1   Overview of Section 2.2

In Section 2.2, we will look at how business organisations are classified. There are four different ways of classifying organisations, as outlined below:

1   by reference to their primary activity
2   by reference to their legal form (sole trader, partnership and company – the latter two having several different kinds), unincorporated associations and trusts
3   by reference to their profit aims
4   by reference to ownership and control.

We shall look at each of the above in turn. Knowing what a business does, the legal form it takes, whether it is profit-oriented and who owns and controls it, etc., provides a wider context for the financial statements it produces, and their format, and may engender certain stakeholder interests in its financial results. Although different legal organisational forms may be subject to different rules as to financial statements and their format, if they keep accounting records, these will be kept using the same kind of bookkeeping as has already been described.

2.2.2   Classification by primary activity

There are many different types of business and organisations, and, consequently, they may be classified in different ways, for example, by reference to a business's primary activity, such as manufacturing (where physical goods are made from raw materials and/or components), transportation (where goods are delivered or people transported), utilities (where services such as fuel, sewage treatment, etc., are provided), education (where teaching or other educational products/ services are provided), and professional services (where legal, banking, accounting, auditing, taxation, investment and other financial services are provided).

Countries often have formal systems of classifying activities, most frequently for companies the shares of which are publicly traded on stock exchanges. This is frequently done by developing a code of numbers with a different number applicable to each industry sector, and may be done by various bodies, such as a stock exchange. The London Stock Exchange, for instance, uses the Standard Industrial Classification (SIC) to determine the main activity of a company, and will assign the same numerical code to all companies which provide the same goods/services. The use of such codes enables users of financial statements to compare results of companies in the same industry. It enables governments to compare statistics of businesses in the home country with those of other countries and develop economic, industrial or even educational policies.

2.2.3   Classification by legal form

One of the commonest ways of classifying organisations is by reference to their legal form, and there are many different legal forms for doing business. Figure 5 below gives a number of forms differentiated by UK law, which are then discussed further. The difference in legal form between some of these relates to the way a particular form of business organisation raises finance, the nature of its activities, its size, how it pays tax and the type of legal and accounting regulations by which it must abide.

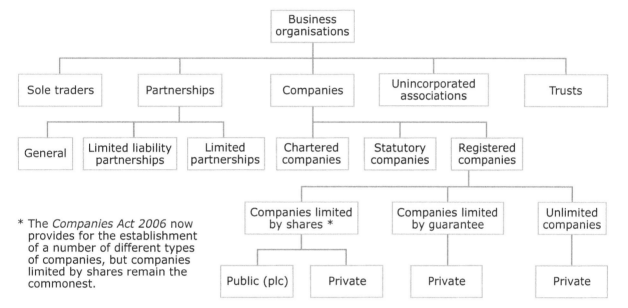

* The *Companies Act 2006* now provides for the establishment of a number of different types of companies, but companies limited by shares remain the commonest.

Figure 5   Different business organisations by reference to legal form

Sole traders (sole proprietors)

These are entities owned by one person, and are the simplest form of business entity to deal with, as there are few formalities or constraints. A sole trader raises finance to do business by investing his/her own money (referred to as capital, equity, etc. – see Section 1.4), borrowing money from friends or obtaining a loan, say, from a bank – or possibly a combination of these things. A sole trader will be personally liable for any debts incurred by the business, so if the business does not generate enough cash to pay business bills as they fall due, the sole trader's personal resources and assets will be used to pay them, and the sole trader may become bankrupt as a result. This is different from limited companies, for example, where the personal resources and assets of investors cannot normally be used to pay company bills. Businesses operated by sole traders tend to be small, because there are limited resources available to their owners. Some are quite literally 'one man' operations, though they can, of course, have employees. Sole traders in general aim to be profit-making, as the business is their primary means of making a living. Sometimes you will see the term sole practitioner used. This term often just means that the person operating a business is offering a service, such as an accountant or a solicitor, rather than selling goods or making them, but is otherwise the same as a sole trader.

The type and format of financial statements are specified by regulations for many entities, but not for sole traders, at least in the UK. However, they would normally prepare rudimentary financial statements to a level that is deemed adequate for taxation purposes, as well as for their own needs. Larger sole traders may choose to produce financial statements in accordance with generally accepted accounting principles (GAAP), which will be referred to later in the unit. There is no legal requirement for a sole trader to have an audit.

Partnerships

General partnerships

A partnership is a business entity owned by two or more persons who each invest resources (typically their own or borrowed money), again referred to as capital (see Section 1.4), and work together with the aim of making a profit. The greater number of owners means that, in comparison with a sole trader, more finance becomes available, and this is a common reason for forming a partnership, but partnership is also a means of sharing the risks of business and managing it. Profits are divided between the partners, often in accordance with the proportions in which they contributed capital to the business, though they can agree to divide profits in any way. Partners often draw up a partnership agreement as a formal written document, which sets out the rules by which the partnership is to be administered and includes things like how profit will be split (to prevent disagreement arising over this). However, there need not be a document – there can also be an oral agreement. If an agreement is silent over profit-sharing arrangements, profits will usually be shared equally. (This is specifically required in the UK by the provisions of the *Partnership Act 1890.*)

The above description is that of a basic general partnership. It is a very old and very common form of doing business worldwide and, in the UK, is governed by one of the oldest pieces of business legislation still applicable: the *Partnership Act 1890*. The partners have authority to act on behalf of the business to bind all the other partners in legal contracts with third parties that are in the ordinary course of the partnership's business. Like sole traders, partners are personally liable for any debts incurred by the partnership, so there is no protection offered to partners' personal assets if the partnership does not generate enough cash to pay bills as they fall due. The partners have a collective (joint) and individual (several) responsibility (or liability) for debts. A partnership will formally end if any partner dies, withdraws or becomes unable to act because of disability. Most partnership agreements will provide for these types of events, and the share of the departed partner is usually purchased by the remaining partners.

All partners usually have an equal right to participate in the management and control of the partnership. Disagreements in the ordinary course of business are decided by a majority of the partners, but disagreements in respect of matters deemed extraordinary, and amendments to the partnership agreement, require that all partners consent to proposed solutions or amendments. In a partnership of any size, the partnership agreement will provide for day to day management of the partnership to be delegated to certain elected partners. Unless otherwise stated in the partnership agreement, no one can become a member of the partnership without the consent of all partners, though a partner is permitted to give (or 'assign') his/her share of the profits and losses to others.

Limited liability partnerships (LLPs)

Until relatively recently, the partnership form was the only form in which certain professionals who offered services, such as accountants, solicitors, etc., could do business. In addition to liability for partnership debts, as explained above, service professionals also face another threat to business, in that they can be sued by dissatisfied clients. Dissatisfaction can arise for many reasons, but becomes potentially actionable at law if a professional should act negligently, resulting in financial loss for a client, which the client would seek to recover legally by taking the negligent professional to court and suing for damages. In the past, claims have been made for very large sums, far in excess of the amount of capital partners had contributed to businesses, and, indeed, in excess of their personal assets. If a dispute comes to court, it means delay in reaching agreement and uncertainty over the level of damages the court might award, hence cases have often been settled by agreement between the disputing parties outside the courts. This was regarded as very unsatisfactory by partnerships, especially the large accounting practices, and resulted in extensive lobbying of governments for a change of law so that the liability of partners could be restricted to the amount of capital they had invested, such that their personal assets were not at risk. This resulted in the *Limited Liability Partnerships Act 2000* (in England, Wales and Scotland) and the *Limited Liability Partnerships Act (Northern Ireland) 2002*, which introduced these desired changes.

The concept of limited liability for partners is now widespread around the world. LLPs are more complicated to set up and operate than general partnerships, as they must meet many of the same requirements as limited companies. (This is discussed further below).

Limited partnerships

A limited partnership is similar to a general partnership except that in addition to one or more general partners, there are one or more limited partners. It was an early attempt to limit the liability of partners in the way that LLPs now do. The general partners are, in all major respects, in the same legal position as partners in a general partnership, that is, they manage the business, and share the profits of the firm in (pre-defined) proportions, and have joint and several liability for the debts of the partnership. Limited partners, however, have limited liability, meaning they are only liable on debts incurred by the firm to the extent of their registered investment, and have no management authority. This latter was the price they paid for having limited liability. The general partners usually pay the limited partners a return on their investment, the nature and extent of which is usually defined in the partnership agreement. It is still theoretically possible to set up a limited partnership, but the form shares and any premium paid in return for the issue of the shares by the company. A shareholder's personal assets are thereby protected if the company cannot generate enough cash to pay its bills and becomes insolvent, but money already invested in the company will be lost. A significant characteristic of a company is that it is a legal person, which means it is separate in the eyes of the law from the people owning or running it (a sole trader is not). It can act in its own name and can make legally binding contracts. It is said thus to have legal personality. An LLP, despite being a partnership, also has legal personality.

Although the personal assets of shareholders are protected, as described above, sometimes this is undermined. In many small companies, typically family-owned companies, the shareholders are also the directors. If such companies apply for loans, lenders commonly make it a condition of granting any loan that the directors personally guarantee that the loans will be repaid if the company itself fails to repay them. While this may be an incentive to the directors to do their best to ensure that the company is profitable, it does mean that their personal assets will be at risk.

A limited company may be private or public. A private limited company is not required by law to disclose as much about its activities and operations as a public company, and can only issue its shares privately. This is the major distinguishing feature between a private limited company and a public limited company, which can issue shares to the general public and trade them on a stock exchange, though it is not compelled to do the latter. Most companies, particularly small companies, are private. If they wish to sell or transfer shares, this will be by a private, not public, sale, and the procedures will be laid down in their Articles of Association. Some countries (e.g., the USA and Malaysia) do permit certain private companies to raise debt finance publicly. In such circumstances, companies in general must comply with the more stringent regulations which apply to public companies in this area.

Private companies limited by shares are required to have the suffix 'Limited' (often written 'Ltd' or 'Ltd.') or 'Incorporated' ('Inc.') as part of their name, though the latter cannot be used in the UK or the Republic of Ireland. In the Republic of Ireland 'Teoranta' ('Teo.') may be used instead, though this is limited mainly to Gaeltacht companies (i.e., companies situated in an Irish-speaking region). 'Cyfyngedig' ('Cyf.') may be used by Welsh companies in a similar fashion.

A public limited company must include the words 'public limited company' or the abbreviation 'p.l.c.' at the end of its name ('Plc', 'plc' and 'PLC' being deemed equally acceptable). In the Republic of Ireland, the upper case initials 'CPT' (Irish: 'cuideachta phoiblí theoranta') may be used instead. In the UK, Welsh companies may use 'c.c.c.' or 'CCC' (Welsh: 'cwmni cyfyngedig cyhoeddus') in place of p.l.c. Certain public limited companies (mostly nationalised concerns), incorporated under special legislation, are exempted from bearing any of the identifying suffixes.

Activity 2.2   ....

Visit the website of the Chartered Institute of Taxation (CIOT), via the link on the B291 website. In the 'site search' box, type in 'royal charter' and navigate through to the CIOT's royal charter, which you will then be able to read. Take about ten minutes to do this.

Feedback   ....

The CIOT was granted a royal charter in 1994, and is one of the most recent instances of this rare form of setting up a chartered company. You will see that the language of the charter is very old-fashioned and may be difficult to understand.

Activity 2.3   ....

Visit the corporate website of Sainsbury's (J Sainsbury plc, the UK-based supermarket) via the link on the B291 website and enter 'annual report' into the search box. You should then find a link to the most recent annual report. It is recommended that you download the annual report as a pdf. You will not need to print the document, but please make sure that you are able to read the pdf on screen. Find the note to the financial statements headed 'Called up share capital and share premium account' and read the details about share capital there (ignore the part of the note which refers to 'movements in the called up share capital and share premium account'). Note down the things you do not understand. Spend no more than 20 minutes on this.

Feedback   ....

This note looks extremely complicated, but it is not, really. First of all, this refers to the shares relevant to one company only, despite it saying 'group' here. You will see that the company is allowed to issue two different sorts of shares – ordinary and preference, with amounts specified. This is referred to as 'authorised share capital', and is the maximum the company can issue (in number of shares and value), though not all of it needs to be issued. Preference shares are ones on which a dividend has to be declared payable every year and before any dividend on ordinary shares, so they are regarded as a less risky type of investment.

The next lines give 'called up share capital – allotted and fully paid ordinary shares' – and this shows how much of the share capital has actually been issued to shareholders (= 'called up' and 'allotted'). No preference shares have been issued and not all of the ordinary share capital. 'Fully paid' means what it says. Sometimes shareholders are asked to pay only a portion of the share value they agree to pay, but they can be asked for the extra at any time by the company.

'Share premium' is the amount shareholders have paid over and above the nominal value of the shares (see above).

Companies limited by guarantee

Under British, Irish and Australian law, a company limited by guarantee is an alternative type of corporation used primarily for non-profit organisations that require legal personality. A company limited by guarantee does not usually have a share capital, but instead has members who are guarantors instead of shareholders. The guarantors give an undertaking to contribute a nominal amount (typically very small) towards the winding up of the company in the event of there being inadequate funds upon cessation of business. A company limited by guarantee must include the suffix 'Limited' in its name, and it is a form commonly used for clubs, membership organisations, including students' unions, sports associations

Trusts

A trust is a formal arrangement set up usually by a document known as a trust deed, whereby assets or money are transferred by one person (the settlor) to one or more others (trustees) to hold, administer, make payments, etc., for the benefit of one or more persons (beneficiaries). Trusts in general are not active business entities, but you may frequently encounter them or hear them being mentioned. Many pension funds, for example, are set up as trusts. There are often specialised regulations governing trust financial statements and we do not go into this topic in B291.

Other types of organisational forms

You may at this point be thinking about other types of organisational forms that you have heard about, such as branches, divisions or groups of companies. Branches and divisions are not separate legal entities, but are subsidiary parts of a larger entity, most often a company, and are usually dedicated to selling or manufacturing a particular product or range of products or delivering a particular service. The financial results of branches and divisions are added in to the main financial statements of the larger body. While it is possible to produce branch or divisional financial statements (and this is often done, especially for management accounting purposes), these are not published externally as separate financial statements, though large companies will disclose detailed information about branches or divisions in the notes to their financial statements.

Groups of companies exist when one company, referred to as a parent company, owns the shares of one or more other companies. You may often see the term holding company used instead of 'parent company' in this context, as both are terms used to denote a company which owns shares in other companies. Typically accounting dictionaries do not differentiate between the two terms, but in practice there may be several differences. While a parent company will always be a holding company, by definition, a holding company may not always be a parent company, as it may just own shares in, say, a sub-group of companies which carry on similar types of business, and may be itself owned by a parent company. Often, too, a parent company may carry out business activities as well as owning shares, whereas a holding company is unlikely to do so: the latter is typically a more 'passive' entity. Holding companies are often used for tax purposes, as, for example, they facilitate in a tax-effective manner the repatriation of income earned outside a group's home jurisdiction.

Where the parent company controls another company (most obviously when it holds more than 50 per cent of the shares carrying voting rights of the other company), the owned companies are referred to as subsidiary companies. If a company is less than 50 per cent owned, the actual percentage and level of control determine whether the owned company will be considered as an associated company or simply as an investment. There are special ways of adding together the results of the parent company, subsidiaries and associates to produce group financial statements (sometimes called consolidated financial statements). We do not in this module teach you how to produce group financial statements (though the process is just an extension of the double-entry bookkeeping you will learn in Units 2 and 3 of B291), but you will learn to understand and use them in Unit 5 (when you learn how to do financial analysis), as most of the companies with shares traded on stock exchanges throughout the world are groups of companies. Some of these groups are very large and contain hundreds, if not thousands of companies, located in different parts of the world. They are often referred to as multinational companies (MNCs) or multinational enterprises (MNEs) (though the latter term is not specifically confined to companies). However, private limited companies can also form groups.

Activity 2.5 ....

Look again at the pdf of the J Sainsbury plc latest annual report that you downloaded in Activity 2.3. This is an example of a set of group financial statements. Take some time (about 20 minutes) to browse through these statements.

Feedback ....

You will no doubt be thinking that this is a long and very complicated document, and be wondering what you have let yourself in for on this module. Do not worry. This is just a 'taster'. By the end of Unit 5, you will feel much more comfortable with published sets of financial statements.

2.2.4 Classification by reference to profit aims

Sometimes organisations are classified in accordance with the principles underlying their chief activity – namely, in accordance with whether they are seeking profits or not. Often non-profit organisations are subject to specialised requirements for the format and presentation of their financial statements. For example, in the UK, charities must generally comply with the requirements of the *Charities Act 2006*, which has specific sections on financial statements. Profit-seeking organisations are typically sole traders, partnerships and companies. These are discussed more fully in Section 2.2.3, under different legal forms. Profit-seeking organisations may have several different objectives. For a very long time, it was generally accepted that maximising the wealth of their owners and continuing in existence were the primary objectives of profit-seeking organisations. However, as organisations also aim, for example, to provide goods and services to customers and employment to employees, it is, perhaps, more reasonable to suggest that increasing, rather than maximising, the wealth of owners, is a more fitting objective. All of the aforementioned objectives do require profit to be made in the longer term. Non-profit organisations, on the other hand, do not see wealth maximisation/increase as their main objective, but seek to satisfy the particular needs of their members or sectors of society. Such organisations are referred to as 'not-for-profit organisations' (NFPs) or 'non-profit organisations' (NPOs), and might include:

- government departments and agencies, for example, in the UK, HM Revenue & Customs (HMRC), the purpose of which will be to implement government policy
- schools, where the chief objective will be the provision of education
- hospitals, where the main aim will be to treat the sick
- charities, where the aim will be to provide relief or benefit, the particular kind depending on the nature of the charity, such as relief of famine or hardship (Oxfam) or educational services (The Open University)
- clubs and societies, where the aim will be to foster the interests of members
- local councils, where the aim will be to provide services, for example, waste collection, street lighting, etc., to a community within a defined area
- mutual organisations (e.g., some building societies, trade unions, and working men's clubs), where services are provided from members' subscriptions to those members.

Activity 2.6

Refer back to Activity 2.4 and revisit the Oxfam website. Also look at HMRC's website, via the link on the B291 website, and find out what they do. Take about ten minutes to do this.

Feedback

Please refer back to Activity 2.4 feedback for details about Oxfam. Note again that it said:

> 'Oxfam GB is a leading international NGO with a worldwide reputation for excellence in the delivery of aid and development work. Our purpose is to work with others to overcome poverty and suffering.'

Oxfam's charitable status was also emphasised.

For HMRC, you should find:

> 'HM Revenue & Customs (HMRC) was formed on the 18 April 2005, following the merger of Inland Revenue and HM Customs and Excise Departments. Work is still continuing on our office restructuring programme. We are here to ensure the correct tax is paid at the right time, whether this relates to payment of taxes received by the department or entitlement to benefits paid.'

(This relates to the UK's tax authority, but most countries have a website for their national tax authority – see, for example, the USA's at www.irs.gov.)

The HMRC page also refers to the following activities:

- collection and administration of direct taxes (such as income tax and corporation tax) and of indirect taxes (such as petroleum revenue duty and **Value Added Tax (VAT)**)
- payment and administration of child benefit, child trust fund and tax credits
- protection of the citizen by enforcement and administration of border and frontier protection, environmental taxes, national minimum wage and recovery of student loans.

(Did you know that HMRC did all this?)

2.2.5 Classification by reference to ownership/control

A final way of classifying organisations is by reference to whether they are in the public or private sector and who owns them. The public sector is concerned with providing government services and will be controlled by government organisations. Although what constitutes 'the public sector' varies from country to country, in general the public sector will include services such as the police, military forces, public roads, etc.

The private sector comprises organisations not controlled by government, so will include business, charities, etc., that are not under national ownership.

Activity 2.7 ....

Revisit Activity 2.4 (including feedback) and Activity 2.6 (including feedback) to see examples of what private and public sector organisations do. Spend about ten minutes doing this.

2.2.6 A final word on organisational classification

The discussion in Section 2.2 about organisational classification applies commonly throughout capitalist economies, as ideas about legal forms in terms of sole traders, partnerships (including limited liability partnerships) and companies limited by shares are valid across different jurisdictions and cultures. While we have not gone into detail about the historical development of these ideas, they are all well established ideas, which have been in existence for a very long time. For example, the modern notion of limited partnership had its origins in the Qirad and Mudaraba institutions in mediaeval Islamic law, and accompanied the development of large scale international business operations. There will, however, be some variations, so one could not expect a limited liability partnership or company in the United States, for instance, to be exactly the same as in England, as under the US system such entities are governed by the laws of 50 states individually. Also, there may be additional, slightly different legal forms. For example, the USA has several different types of corporate entity with different degrees of limited liability that are subject to different tax regulations, which is a crucial difference between them. While different legal systems implement concepts differently, the underlying concepts, however, remain the same.

2.3 Functions of accounting in different types of organisations

In Section 1.1.2 you learned that accounting is a process which identifies, organises, classifies, records, summarises and communicates information about economic events, usually, but not exclusively, in monetary terms. The same kind of bookkeeping will be done by any kind of entity, but the functions of financial accounting will vary between different types of organisation, and may be influenced by their size and legal form.

All organisations will need to know if they have made a profit/surplus or not. This is a very important function of accounting. For a non-profit-seeking organisation, like a charity, this will show if it has expended too little on its charitable objectives. For profit-seeking organisations (sole traders, partnerships and most types of companies) this will be the starting point for working out how much tax will be payable to the tax authorities.

Knowing how much profit has been made is important in terms of how much a sole trader and partners may withdraw from their business – hence, it can have a direct effect on their quality and style of living. Similarly, it is important for companies to decide how much profit can be paid out to shareholders by way of dividends. Branches and divisions will need to know if they, as part of a larger body, are making sufficient profits to ensure their survival. Financial accounting profit may be important for deciding branch or division management bonuses – similarly for the larger body to which they belong.

Profit that is not taken out of a sole tradership or partnership or paid out as dividends by a company will be retained by the business. This will help the business grow and invest in new assets or opportunities. Therefore, there is a balance to be struck between paying out or withdrawing profit and retaining it within the business. For companies, there are legal restrictions governing how much profit may be distributed as dividends, but no such restrictions apply to profits withdrawn by sole traders or partnerships.

Formally drawing up a balance sheet shows the financial position of a business at the end of an accounting period, and will show the value of assets and liabilities. If assets are included on the balance sheet, this is prima facie evidence of their existence and value. Existence and value are especially important if a business has bank or other formal loans, as loans might be secured on one or more of the assets. Formally drawing up a balance sheet will show whether or not such assets are still owned by the business, and their physical condition should be reflected in their stated value. Banks which have loaned money to a business may routinely want to see its financial statements to make sure that assets on which a loan is secured still exist, and have not been sold; to see that a loan is likely to be repaid; to ensure that enough profit is made to cover interest payments due; and to check generally that conditions under which a loan was made have not been breached. The existence of formal procedures to check on the existence and value of assets is also likely to discourage theft and embezzlement. Moreover, if a business is applying for a loan, a lender will want to see up to date financial statements (as well as various types of management accounting information).

Some business entities, most typically large public companies, the shares of which are traded on a stock exchange, produce financial statements every three or six months, as well as annually. Such financial statements are referred to as interim financial statements and are often required as a result of the shares being publicly traded. Their purpose is to inform investors and financial markets in general about what is happening in the company. Public companies are also required to issue profit warnings if their profits are not expected to be in line with forecasts.

2.4 Users' and stakeholders' needs

One of the main functions of financial accounting is to communicate information to interested parties. We look in this section at the specific needs of various users and stakeholders and examine how financial accounting information, as shown in income statements, balance sheets and accompanying notes, can address those needs. Some users and stakeholders have a direct interest in an organisation because of a degree of personal involvement of some kind, that is, they run or work for the organisation (such as management and employees) or have invested personal money in it (such as shareholders in a company). Other stakeholders' interests may be financial, for example, an interest in the ability of the business to meet various financial liabilities, or may be focused on the effect of the business's activities on society and the environment. Depending on the nature of the stakeholder, the interest may still be quite personal in terms of effect on a particular person/ entity, or it may be more remote. Stakeholder theory is a term often given to such a wider attempt to consider the interests of all stakeholders in a business, rather than focusing on the narrower idea that a business is responsible only to its owners (often referred to as shareholder theory in the context of companies). You should also note that accounting information, as shown in published financial statements of companies, for example, is heavily regulated, and some of that regulation is in place to ensure that certain user needs (e.g., those of shareholders) are met. Figure 6 below shows typical users and stakeholders with an interest in public company financial accounting information.

Figure 6   Different users and stakeholders with an interest in public company financial statements

2.4.10   Special interest groups

There may be special interest groups which are very interested in one or more aspects of a business. An example might be an environmental body interested in how a chemical company disposes of toxic waste or a firm of financial analysts which gives investment advice to clients.

Activity 2.8 ....

In which category of users or stakeholders do you think the following fit?

1   Greenpeace
2   Ms Brown, the managing director of Zip Ltd
3   Mr Jones, who is thinking about buying some shares in Sainsbury's
4   Mr Smith, who is one of Zip Ltd's sales representatives

Spend about ten minutes on this.

Feedback ....

1   Special interest group – Greenpeace is an environmental pressure group.

2   The managing director is part of the management stakeholder group, but as managing director, if she is a competent and conscientious director, she will also be concerned about ensuring that other stakeholders' needs are addressed.

3   Mr Jones is a potential shareholder of Sainsbury's, so he will fall into the shareholder group.

4   Mr Smith is one of Zip Ltd's employee stakeholders.

Summary

In this session you have learned about the context of accounting, with a focus on different organisations' objectives and different ways of classifying organisations (by reference to primary activity, legal form, profit aims and ownership/control), and how this can be important for accounting purposes. You have also learned about various functions of accounting and different users' and stakeholders' perspectives and needs.

In Session 3 we will go on to look at the wider, external context of accounting by helping you to understand how accounting has developed and the ways in which environmental factors influence or place constraints on the development of business and accounting practices. We will thus consider political and legal factors; macroeconomic and fiscal policy; financial and capital market issues; and social, demographic, technological, professional and regulatory influences.

SESSION **3 Environmental influences and constraints on business and accounting**

Introduction

Upon completion of Session 3 you are expected to be able to:

- explain briefly the history and development of accounting and finance in business
- indicate how environmental influences (such as political, legal, economic, social, demographic and technological factors) impact on business and accounting
- relate the development of financial and capital markets to the need for reliable and relevant accounting information and the development of financial accounting standards
- describe the organisation of the accounting profession in the UK
- explain how regulatory frameworks and the organisation of the accounting profession influence the development of accounting standards, rules and practices
- describe the accounting regulatory framework in the UK
- describe the international accounting regulatory structure and the International Accounting Standards Board (IASB).

In Session 3 you will learn about the history and role of accounting in business and the various environmental influences and constraints on business (such as political and legal factors, macroeconomic factors and social, demographic and technological influences), as well as financial and capital markets. These provide the wider context in which both organisations and accountants operate. In addition, you will learn about the further regulatory constraints governing the work of accountants within that wider context, including the organisation of the profession.

3.1 The history and development of accounting and finance in business

Accounting for private business dates back to the origins of capitalist organisations. History points to auditors and accountants developing together. The earliest records show that information was recorded using simple stone and wood devices (see Table 2). Then, in Ancient Egypt, the introduction of papyrus (paper) and ink made recording information quicker and easier.

investors and entrepreneurs. For example, Italian merchants engaging in trade with the Middle East and Far East needed to know the financial state of affairs of people who came to them for loans or funding. It was the need to control financial relationships between these merchants and their creditors and investors that led to the development of banking and double-entry records and reports.

Much later, during the Industrial Revolution (in the eighteenth and nineteenth centuries in England), a tendency developed to employ accountants, sometimes known as public accountants, to perform various financial functions, including installing bookkeeping systems for new enterprises as well as winding up failed companies, that is, sorting out the affairs of companies which had become insolvent and were unable to pay their bills. The concept of auditing became important towards the end of the nineteenth century, as shareholders who did not participate in day to day management of companies needed assurance that investee companies were being properly run.

The first person in Western Europe considered to have practised auditing on a full time basis was a Scotsman named George A. Watson, who was born in 1645 in Edinburgh. As the need for common criteria for accounting practice became more important, public accounting grew to be regulated by professional institutes, societies and associations. By the end of the nineteenth century, accounting bodies had emerged. Their role was to establish, design and manage written examinations and quantitative grading as a way of regulating the entry of new people to the profession of public accountant, and assuring the provision of high quality accounting services – therefore, allowing accounting firms to develop good reputations.

More on the history of accounting and accountants

This discussion of the history of accounting and accountants is necessarily brief. Further relevant material can be found at http://www.acaus.org where the paper by John R. Alexander, entitled 'The History of Accounting', may be freely downloaded. A link to this paper will also be provided on the B291 website.

The 'professionalisation' of accounting and auditing reflected developments that were taking place in the management of enterprises. Once reliant on the skills of the entrepreneur, management moved towards a scientific approach that could be learned and taught. Today, the accounting profession is itself an international industry which gives clients advice on a wide range of different issues, some of which derive from the nature of the business they do, while others arise from the need to deal with and account for the external influences and constraints of the environments in which they operate. Sections 3.2–3.5 consider these environmental influences and constraints.

3.2 Environmental influences

3.2.1 Introduction

Organisations will carry out analyses of their external environment as part of their overall business planning to identify the constraints under which they must operate, to identify potential threats and opportunities, and often to determine whether they will need professional accounting or business advice to deal with them. Generally, the major environmental factors impacting on an organisation can be grouped under four headings: **p**olitical/legal, **e**conomic, **s**ocial/demographic and **t**echnological (reflected in the acronym, PEST analysis). These factors will be considered in greater depth in Units 1 and 7 of B292, but the brief outline given here is adequate for the purposes of B291.

3.2.2 Political and legal factors

The political systems of countries in which organisations operate will impact on them in various ways. The prevailing political ideology of the government of a given sovereign state may mean that business can only operate in a certain way, such as being state owned under certain socialist regimes. Some governments might set up trade barriers to prevent goods being exported or imported and/or not allow businesses from overseas to operate within their jurisdictions.

The laws and regulations which governments implement affect ways of doing business, for example, in terms of the law of tort, contract law or company law, which regulate different aspects of business behaviour, such as negligence, how deals are made, how financial statements should be presented and what they should contain. Tax law, too, is important in that it determines how much tax a business will need to pay on its profits, but it can also be used to offer incentives to businesses to undertake certain activities in preference to others (e.g., set up an operation in a low employment area by giving various tax allowances or subsidies). Other areas of law that generally affect organisations are employment law, health and safety legislation, consumer protection legislation, environmental legislation and data protection legislation.

The sources of law depend on whether a country operates under a system of common law or codified law. In a common law jurisdiction (such as the UK, USA, Australia, Canada and New Zealand), the sources of law are generally national Acts of Parliament, decisions of senior courts (e.g., the Supreme Court in the UK and the USA), and other major courts through the principles of case law and setting of legal precedents. Sometimes, too, there are regional sources of law (such as bye-laws issued by local councils in the UK or individual state laws in the USA). The decisions of courts and principles developed in case law are of particular importance in common law jurisdictions, as law develops incrementally in accordance with decisions made in certain courts, and is not all embodied in particular statutes. In the UK, for example, much of contract law is based on common law. In codified law systems, such as those in much of continental Europe, law is

Fiscal policy impacts on businesses in the form of the taxes they must pay, which they need to be able to calculate, for which they will need to put appropriate entries through their books and which, if appropriate, they may need to report in their financial statements. Depending on their legal form, size, type of activity, etc., businesses may have to deal with a variety of taxes, for example, income tax, corporation tax, business rates, capital gains tax and Value Added Tax (VAT). They will also need to collect employment taxes from employees' wages to pay to the tax authority in due course. (Unit 3 will look at VAT and taxes on wages in more detail.) Complying with tax legislation creates a burden for businesses in terms of administration, and often, additional costs if they need to obtain professional help from a tax adviser to ensure that all requirements are met, as these can be complex. Part of this complexity lies in the technical difficulty associated with calculations, but much of it derives from the fact that individual taxes often have a long history, and the ways that they are applied, and to whom or to what, continually change.

'The best way to boost the economy is to lower taxes. The best way to lower your taxes is to reduce your income. Paying you less is my patriotic duty!'

Monetary policy

Monetary policy refers to the management of the economy's money supply, which is the total amount of money in the economy. There are many different ways of estimating this. Monetary policy involves measures either to increase the total supply of money in the economy (an expansionary policy) or to decrease it (a contractionary policy). There are several measures which can be used to different effect, namely changing interest rates, setting reserve requirements for banks, or trading in open and foreign exchange markets. Controlling the money supply in these ways is also referred to as monetarism or monetarist theory.

Attempts to control the money supply have an impact on businesses in terms of the availability of money to borrow. If it is difficult to borrow money, either because lenders are unwilling to lend, or because interest rates are high (both contractionary effects), businesses may be unable to continue to operate. Lack of funds to borrow may also compel businesses to turn to other sources of funding, such as retained earnings. In general, harsh economic times may push businesses into trying to show their results in the best possible light and the use of 'creative' accounting techniques to achieve this (see Section 3.6).

3.2.4 Social and demographic factors

Social factors relate to the impact of societal structure and changes on business. For example, the existence of different groups within society (as defined by income, education, profession, etc.) creates the potential for different customer groups with different demands (e.g., single parent families requiring low cost housing or child care for parents in work). Changes in people's attitudes, values and lifestyles will also create different demands, for example, greater awareness of the food we eat and where it comes from in terms of animal well-being, also greater concern about environmental issues, such as 'greenhouse' gases. A concern about environmental issues could translate into a changed attitude to the recycling of waste (to minimise use of landfill for rubbish and use of plastic to provide packaging products, etc.). Changes in tastes and fashions can also have an adverse effect on organisations which do not anticipate changes or do not accept them. Clothes, cars and items such as mobile phones are examples of things subject to such changes, and organisations which make or supply them must be able to adapt to survive.

Demographic factors relate to the population and groups within it. It is important for organisations to know about population size, and its composition and location. An increasing population size may, for example, indicate a growing market and availability of a workforce. Birth rates, death rates, immigration and emigration will determine population growth or decline, and these things vary across the world. Rates of birth and death also determine the age profile of a population. Some countries have noticeable imbalances, with, say, a relatively young population (making them attractive to firms needing a large workforce) or an older one (creating problems with availability of pensions). Where a population lives and how densely it is packed together are also significant. There is an increasing proportion of the world's population living in cities, which has various implications for the type of goods and services they might need and consequently for the organisations which might provide them.

The amount of disposable income which people have, their level of education and their health also significantly affect businesses in terms of the luxury goods they might buy, the skills present in the workforce, and, indeed, the availability of that workforce in the first instance. For example, the incidence of HIV/AIDS in sub-Saharan African countries, notably South Africa, means a changed population structure with fewer people in middle age – normally the most economically active group, and one which supports elderly and young people. In many Western countries, eating habits and obesity are a major concern, which has implications for the 'fast food' industry. Health issues also create greater demands on the medical profession and healthcare providers generally.

to financial statements, so it is important for accountants to know and understand the nature of financial and capital markets and institutions.

3.3.2   The nature and role of financial markets

A financial market, as the definition above implies, is a place where those who wish to borrow or raise capital can meet those who are willing to provide it. There are two main types of financial market:

1   Primary markets. These deal in new issues of finance, such as issues of new shares or debentures.

2   Secondary markets. These deal in trading of what might be termed 'second-hand' or 'pre-owned' financial assets of various kinds, for example, securities, bonds, debentures/loan stock. They do not provide new funds, but allow holders of existing assets to sell them on to other investors. It is thought that a well developed secondary market should reduce price volatility of traded assets through regular trading activities.

A stock exchange is, by definition, a secondary market as it does not deal with the issue of new shares or debentures. Before shares or debentures can be traded on a stock exchange, they must first be listed as a separate exercise by satisfying that exchange's listing requirements. Once listed, shares and debentures may be bought and sold. The London Stock Exchange in the UK, for example, deals in two major types of security – company securities (shares and long-term loan stock/debentures) and public sector stocks. (We will look below in more detail at the role of a stock exchange and at the London Stock Exchange as an example of a stock exchange.) London is also a major market for international bonds (e.g., eurobonds). International bonds are issued to raise debt finance in different countries by governments, supranational organisations, banks and large companies. There is also a London money market, although there is no physical market place, as transactions are conducted by telephone, telex or electronically.

3.3.3   The role of a stock exchange

Most people have heard of the London Stock Exchange as it is one of the oldest and most famous in the world, and still one of the most important. The word 'stock' is an old word for a number of different things and can mean commodities, business capital or money invested in a commercial enterprise, and also property held for public purposes by a nation, so it is not surprising to see it used in this way to refer to a financial market. 'Stock' is also a common term for US ordinary shares. It should not in this context be confused with the concept of trading stock, which we refer to in this module as 'inventory'. 'Share' is a term which reflects the concept that capital can be divided.

Most countries with well developed and internationally operative financial systems have a stock exchange. A stock exchange, as we have seen, is essentially a market for trading in certain types of shares and debt securities – the issued shares of public companies, government bonds, local authority and other publicly owned institution loans and some foreign company stocks. There may be more than one type of stock market in operation in any one country. In the UK, for example, there are three stock markets:

1   The London Stock Exchange (LSE). As mentioned above, this deals in two major types of security including the shares of large public companies. However, it is a complex and expensive process for a company to 'go public', that is, get its shares listed on a stock exchange. Therefore, there are two additional stock markets:

2   The Alternative Investment Market (AIM). This is another arm of the London Stock Exchange, but is a junior market for the shares of smaller companies unwilling or unready for a full listing on the main market.

3   The Over The Counter Market (OTC). This is a market in which financial assets, including shares, are traded other than through a formal stock exchange (e.g., by telephone and e-mail) as there are no physical market premises. Most OTC trading is done by large institutional investors (like pension funds – see below) between themselves. The world's largest OTC market is the National Association of Securities Dealers Automated Quotations Systems (NASDAQ) in the USA.

Few investors would be willing to risk buying shares or lending money if they could not easily sell such long-term investments. The saleability of such investments is an essential characteristic, which is why public companies cannot proceed with an issue of their shares unless they know that they are acceptable to the relevant stock exchange(s). A stock exchange thus plays a crucial role in the provision of capital to industry. If a company has a good reputation with investors, its shares tend to increase in value, and it usually finds it easy to raise capital through an issue of new shares, and thus grow. This is not the case for every company.

Most UK public company shares which are listed on a stock exchange are now held by what are termed institutional investors, meaning pension funds, insurance companies (in life assurance funds) and open-ended investment companies (OEICs). The UK government has, however, tried to encourage wider private ownership of shares by privatising a number of government-owned organisations and encouraging employees and small investors to buy shares. One of the first government organisations affected was the Post Office, when its telecommunications arm was separated out from mail services and subsequently privatised. The privatisation of many other utilities followed. The government also encourages private investment by enabling people to invest certain sums annually in shares with no tax consequences. An example is the stocks and shares Individual Savings Account (ISA), where dividend income and capital gains are free of tax. Such accounts are provided by a variety of financial institutions.

Sometimes share prices in a particular company or in general are affected by the activities of speculators. A speculator deals in shares with a view to making a quick profit from favourable price movements. This might seem a little like betting which assets will go up in price and which will go down.

country), some of which still specialise in different kinds of accounting. Most countries now have at least one main accounting body or institute.

The accounting bodies in the UK played a significant role in the establishment of the Accounting Standards Committee (ASC) in the 1960s, the first body set up to develop accounting standards. This has played an important role in UK accounting regulation. Since the establishment in the UK of the Financial Reporting Council (FRC) as an independent regulatory body in the 1990s (see Section 3.6), the Accounting Standards Board (the successor to the ASC) does not have such a prominent a role. However, it still has considerable input into – and influence on – the setting of accounting standards and regulations at both national and international levels, through formal consultation of its members. The fact that four very large firms of (financial) accountants (KPMG, Ernst & Young, PricewaterhouseCoopers and Deloitte) currently have corporate membership of certain accounting bodies, such as the ICAEW, and the fact that they are multinational enterprises, contributes towards the influence held by accounting bodies in general. Despite many attempts made over the years by the different UK institutes to merge into a smaller number of bodies, they remain primarily organised by the type of accounting practised or their location.

Activity 3.2 ....

How many UK professional accounting bodies can you name? Write them down, trying to group them according to the type of accounting in which they specialise. Spend no more than 15 minutes on this.

Feedback ....

How many did you manage to list? Did you know that there are six chartered accounting bodies? If you are interested in becoming an accountant, you may have already decided which one you hope to join. You will find links to the websites of all the UK bodies at www.accountingeducation.com if you wish to have more information about them.

So far as classifying them is concerned, you may have come up with a list like the following.

Financial accountants
● The Association of Chartered Certified Accountants (ACCA) [www.accaglobal.com and www.acca.org.uk for the UK site]
● The Institute of Chartered Accountants of Scotland (ICAS) [www.icas.org.uk]
● The Institute of Chartered Accountants in England and Wales (ICAEW) [www.icaew.com]
● Chartered Accountants Ireland (formerly the Institute of Chartered Accountants in Ireland (ICAI)), considered to be both a British and Irish professional body (it predates the Partition of Ireland in 1922) [www.charteredaccountants.ie]

Management accountants
● The Chartered Institute of Management Accountants (CIMA) [www.cimaglobal.com]

Note that members of the ACCA, ICAS and ICAEW also work as management accountants in commerce and industry, so these bodies should be included here as well (though they do not indicate this specialism in their names as CIMA does).

Public sector accountants
- The Chartered Institute of Public Finance and Accountancy (CIPFA) [www.cipfa.org.uk]

There are five main chartered accountancy bodies that specialise in the private sector and a sixth (CIPFA) that specialises in the public sector.

There are also lower level accounting qualifications, including:
- The Association of Accounting Technicians (AAT) [www.aat.co.uk] and several additional bodies which accountants (and non-qualified accountants) can join, including:
- The Chartered Institute of Taxation (CIOT) [www.tax.org.uk]
- The Institute of Internal Auditors – United Kingdom (IIA–UK) [www.iia.org.uk]
- The Institute of Chartered Secretaries and Administrators (ICSA) [www.icsa.org.uk] (Note that the term 'Secretaries' relates to 'Company Secretaries'.)

You need to pass the examinations of the relevant institutes in order to join any specific bodies. The *Professional Certificate in Accounting* will enable you to gain exemptions from some of the examinations of some of these bodies. You will find the latest information on the exemptions available to holders of the *Professional Certificate in Accounting* on The Open University website. You should note that not all countries have as many different accounting bodies as the UK, or draw distinctions between different accounting specialisms in the same way.

3.5 The general need for a regulatory framework

In Section 3.5, we shall be looking at the need for a regulatory framework in accounting and financial reporting and how that has developed and the reasons underlying that development. We chiefly concentrate here on companies as business entities most affected by this type of regulation. As mentioned in Session 2, sole traders and partnerships are not governed in the same way by accounting and financial reporting regulations.

You have already learned that different classes of user are interested in financial statements, but do not have financial statements that are put together especially for them, that is, copies of the same set of financial statements are given to everyone. As a result, the banker, the customer, the prospective buyer of the business, the supplier, the owner, the employee, etc., all see the same income statement, balance sheet and cash flow statement.

Financial statements must provide a basic minimum of information upon which everyone can rely. While this makes it easier for the accountant to prepare the financial statements, it is not ideal as the interests of each user group are different and each needs different kinds of information from that wanted by the others. The financial statements must, therefore, be something of a compromise and, at the very least, they must provide a basic minimum of information upon which each user group can rely.

Activity 3.3

Spend a few minutes writing down why it is important that all the user groups (stakeholders) are able to rely on the financial statements. Spend about 15 minutes on this.

published some years ago called *Accounting for Growth*, Terry Smith, a stock market analyst, showed how widespread this problem had become. The book revealed just how great the effect upon profits could be if different subjective views were adopted when preparing the financial statements.

Activity 3.5

Read the introduction to the first edition of *Accounting for Growth* (published in 1992), which is available via the B291 website. While you do this, take careful notes of each of the examples of the manipulation of financial information that the author presents. Spend up to 30 minutes on this.

You will possibly find some of the language and terminology a bit complex. Do not worry too much about that. Skip over any terms about which you are unsure. You will still be able to follow enough of the reading to get the point he is making.

©1998 Bill Monroe
www.MonroeArtist.com

'However, by using an alternate method of accounting...'

Feedback

One of the noticeable things about *Accounting for Growth* is that it was published over 20 years after the professional accounting bodies began issuing accounting standards in the 1970s. What happened, in effect, was that as the rules were developed, so some accountants became skilled at finding loopholes and ways around them that allowed their companies to look better than they ought to in their financial statements. In order to deal with this, the UK professional accounting bodies have issued over 50 different accounting standards, and virtually all the first 25 have now been revised or replaced with more precise sets of rules.

In an effort to improve observation of accounting standards, company law was amended to require anyone preparing financial statements for publication outside the business to observe the rules laid down in the accounting standards.

In 1990, the accountancy bodies replaced the Accounting Standards Committee with the Accounting Standards Board (ASB). It took over the SSAPs that were still in use. Accounting standards developed by the ASB are called Financial Reporting Standards (usually abbreviated to FRSs or still referred to as 'Accounting Standards'). The ASB may issue pronouncements other than FRSs, announcing as each one appears what authority, scope and application it will have.

Activity 3.6

In keeping with the desire that financial statements should be useful to all user groups, virtually all the SSAPs and FRSs were written to focus upon providing rules to regulate the financial statements of the most complex businesses as, by default, that would ensure coverage of the least complex.

Can you think of any problems this might have brought for smaller businesses? Spend about ten minutes writing down your views on this.

Feedback

Quite often, the accounting standards required quite detailed processes to be followed and complex calculations to be undertaken. For a large company, these were not likely to have very serious cost implications as their computer systems were often sophisticated enough to deal with any adjustments. However, for smaller businesses, many of which had no sophisticated computing facilities, the costs of complying with the regulations could be very much greater than the costs of not complying with them, yet the smaller companies had to comply, or find a good excuse for not doing so.

Partly to address this point, some of the clauses in standards and even some of the standards themselves, do not apply to smaller businesses. However, the conditions for exemption were usually arbitrary ones based on company size that may have been relevant when accounting was mainly a manual exercise, but are hardly relevant in a modern computerised accounting environment. Also, the users of small business accounting information are unlikely to be greatly concerned about the implications of complex accounting standards.

To correct the situation, the ASB has issued a third category of standard – the Financial Reporting Standard for Smaller Entities (FRSSE). It contains a collection of some of the rules from virtually all the other accounting standards. Small companies can choose whether to apply it or, if they feel it appropriate to do so, continue to apply all the other accounting standards.

SSAPs, FRSs and the FRSSE are known collectively as 'Accounting Standards'. Accounting standards must comply with the laws of the UK and with the Directives of the European Union. The UK *Companies Act 2006* also applies to all UK companies.

At the same time the ASB was formed, a Review Panel was established to monitor published financial statements: the Financial Reporting Review Panel (FRRP). It is empowered under civil law to prosecute companies that fail to comply with the requirements of an accounting standard or company law. No such monitoring process exists for partnership and sole trader financial statements. You can see more about the ASB and the FRC at either www.asb.org.uk or www.frc.org.uk (both URLs link to the same website).

The organisational structure of which the ASB is part is shown in Figure 7a. The ASB operates under the supervision of the FRC, the objectives of which are to:

- guide the ASB on work programmes and issues of public concern
- ensure that work on accounting standards is properly financed
- act proactively as a public influence for securing good accounting practice.

There are several other bodies in Figure 7a, which are likewise supervised by the FRC. These bodies are concerned with audit, actuarial matters (related to pensions), professional accounting practice (the Professional Oversight Board) and corporate governance. For accounting standards, while the ASB is responsible for developing, issuing and withdrawing standards, the Urgent Issues Task force (UITF) is responsible for issuing swift guidance where there are differing interpretations of SSAPs and FRSs and dealing with emerging issues on a temporary basis.

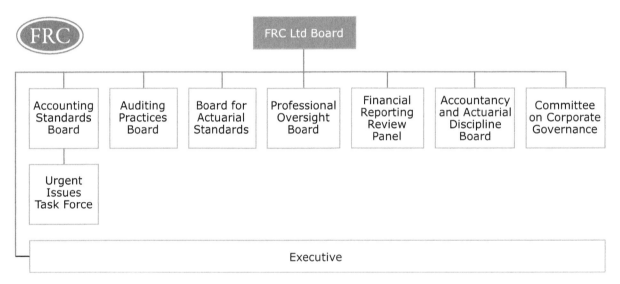

Figure 7a   Accounting regulation – organisation chart

In March 2012 there was a proposal to change the way the FRC operates and a new structure was proposed (see Figure 7b). Under this proposal, the FRC will be supported by three committees:

- the Codes & Standards Committee (advised by the Accounting Council, the Audit & Assurance Council and the Actuarial Council)
- the Conduct Committee (supported by sub-committees on its monitoring and supervising work and on disciplinary matters)
- an Executive Committee.

The proposals for reform can be viewed on the FRC website, which you can access via a link on the B291 website.

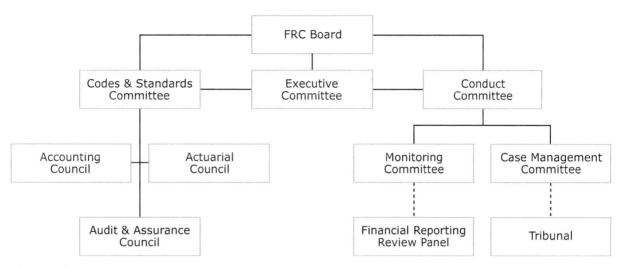

Figure 7b   Proposed FRC structure

3.7 International Financial Reporting Standards and the International Accounting Standards Board

In 1973, the International Accounting Standards Committee (IASC) was founded. This committee consisted of representatives from about 15 accountancy bodies across the world, representing seven countries.

Activity 3.7

Why do you think the IASC was formed? Spend about ten minutes writing down a list of possible reasons.

Feedback

The IASC was formed in order to encourage standardisation in the methods applied when preparing accounting statements to:

● make international investment decisions more compatible

● reduce the costs of converting financial statements made under one regime of accounting regulation to comply with those prepared under another (by multinational companies)

● encourage the growing number of national standard-making bodies to work in harmony

● provide accounting standards for countries that do not have their own standard-setting bodies.

The IASC was reorganised and its standard-setting arm became the International Accounting Standards Board (IASB) in 2001. You can find more details of the IASB on its website at www.iasb.org. The operational structure of the IASB is illustrated in Figure 8.

While the IASB is an independent body, with overall responsibility for creating IFRSs, it is appointed and overseen by a geographically and professionally diverse group of trustees (Trustees of the IFRS Foundation) who are accountable to the public interest. It is also supported by an advisory council and an interpretations committee (IFRIC) and SME Implementation Group to offer guidance where divergence in practice occurs. The actual standard-setting process is outlined in Figure 9.

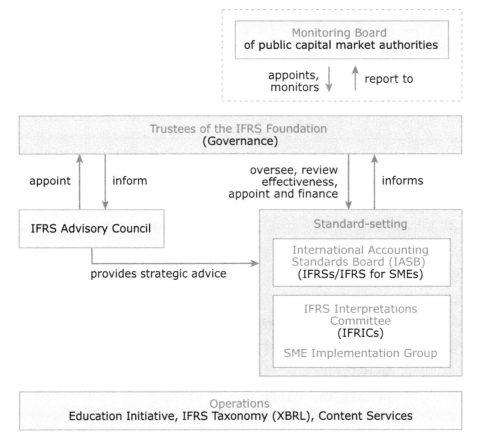

Figure 8   Organisation of the IASB

As indicated above, IFRSs are prepared by the IASB. The terminology here can be confusing because the accounting standards produced by the predecessor to the IASB, the International Accounting Standards Committee, are known as International Accounting Standards (IASs) whereas those produced by the IASB are known as IFRSs. However, the IASB adopted the IASs produced by its predecessor. Therefore, for the purposes of this module, when we refer to the body of international accounting standards we will generally refer to them as IFRSs, but if we refer to individual standards we will give them their individual name.

The move towards the use of IFRSs which have been approved by the European Union (EU) means that these accounting standards now automatically become part of company law because they have been adopted by the EU on the basis of a regulation. However, in the UK, IFRSs currently only apply to the financial statements of groups of companies with either debt or equity securities listed on any regulated market of any Member State. It is likely that their use will eventually be extended to apply to the financial statements of all companies.

EU countries already have the option to require compliance with IFRSs by all companies. The UK has chosen not to do this yet, but has decided to permit companies the securities of which are publicly traded to also use IFRSs in their individual company accounts, not just their group accounts, and to permit other companies to use IFRSs in both their group and individual accounts if they wish. Therefore, many companies now have to choose between UK accounting standards and IFRSs – they are not allowed to 'cherry

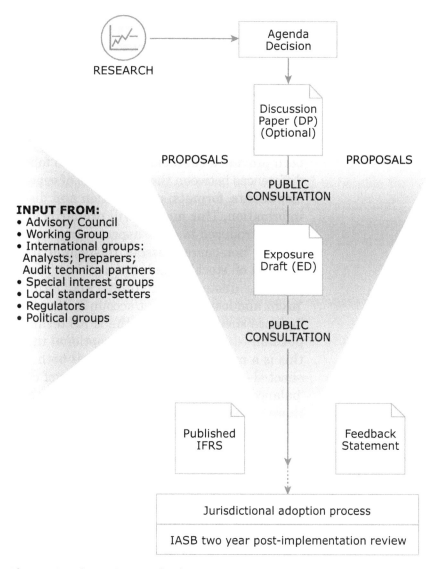

Figure 9   The IASB standard-setting process

pick' from the more favourable aspects of both. It seems likely that where an individual company is part of a group of companies that reports using IFRSs, it will make sense for that individual company to use IFRSs too. Also, it is likely that private companies that want to list in due course on the London Stock Exchange will choose to follow IFRSs. The ASB, however, is heading towards making IFRSs compulsory for medium-sized companies and the FRSSE for smaller companies. Therefore, other private companies may adopt IFRSs in due course.

Even though most UK companies do not have to comply with the requirements of IFRSs yet, UK accounting standards will change significantly in the next few years. As the IASB improves existing international standards and publishes new ones, the UK Accounting Standards Board is bringing the provisions of UK standards substantially into line with IFRSs in a parallel consultation process and reform programme. UK company law has also been modified to incorporate some of the changes following the introduction of IFRSs so that companies, which are either required to adopt IFRSs or which choose to do so, will not be in contravention of the law as a result.

protecting accountants against claims of negligence by providing a set of uniform standards to which they could adhere)

- to address particular financial matters, by providing a response to a crisis in an ad hoc, pragmatic way, or to a longer-term issue, such as inflation and changing prices.

Like the UK, many countries developed their own individual accounting standards. However, as the world's economy has become more globalised, the need to deal with these issues on a global basis has grown, for example, accountants and users of a company's financial statements respectively need to provide and receive a consistent view of results – regardless of the 'home country' of the company, accountant or user. IFRSs are one way in which these issues are being addressed, but their development has been accompanied by an interest in developing a wider conceptual or theoretical framework against which standards might evolve, by setting out general principles inherently capable of dealing with political, fiscal, economic and commercial changes and of eliminating conceptual inconsistencies between different countries. The process of developing standards one by one had hitherto not allowed for broader consideration of accounting theory, and it is only with the benefit of hindsight that one can discern how accounting theory actually evolved.

4.1.2   Evolution of accounting theory

Elliott and Elliott, in their book *Financial Accounting and Reporting*,[1] outline three stages in the evolution of accounting theory:

1   **An empirical inductive approach**. This approach existed prior to 1970, and examined accounting practices that were then in existence, and attempted to generalise and rationalise from them. This resulted in standards that tried to establish best current practice as normal practice, and resulted in, for example, general acceptance of the historical cost model and concepts such as matching and realisation, which will be covered later in Session 4. This approach has played a significant part in the development of accounting/financial reporting practice. However, after the 1970s an increasing rate of economic, political, fiscal and commercial change meant that practices to deal with such developments themselves also changed rapidly, so the process of generalisation from existing practice was no longer pragmatic. Also, there were theoretical issues about how accountants defined income under this approach, which was not the same as how others, such as economists, would define it. Thus the approach was deficient in addressing different user needs.

2   **A deductive approach**. This approach was followed in the 1970s. It resulted in standards which were based on principles deduced from assumptions, for example, that financial statements adjusted for changing prices/inflation would be more appropriate than if prepared on another basis. However, this approach was felt to be unrealistic as it produced figures (especially for income) that were not easily validated and not

[1] Elliott, B. and Elliott, J. (2009) *Financial Accounting and Reporting* (13th edn), Harlow, Essex, Pearson Education Limited.

easily understood by users, as there were several different methods that could be used to adjust for price changes. There was also a problem caused by the nature of the deductive principles being used, as these were basically derived from theoretical economics, and many practising accountants were unhappy about this.

3 **A conceptual framework based on decision-usefulness**. This approach was promoted in the 1980s. According to Elliott and Elliott (2009, p. 160):

> 'It was recognised that standards needed to be decision-useful, that they should satisfy cost/benefit criteria and that their implementation could only be achieved by consensus. Consensus was generally only achievable where there was a clearly perceived rationale underpinning a standard and, even so, alternative treatments were required in order to gain support'.

This 'decision-usefulness' approach has also been used during the twenty-first century, but it is a mandatory model where alternative treatments are not allowed. However, it must be stressed that it is only one of several conceptual frameworks that are possible. Others might be a distributional framework (focusing primarily on stakeholders) or a valuation framework (based on economic principles). The extant conceptual frameworks are considered below.

4.2 Conceptual frameworks: the IASB Conceptual Framework for Financial Reporting (= IASB Framework)

4.2.1 Background

The IASB Framework was originally developed by the (then) IASC in the 1980s, issued in 1989 and adopted by the IASB in April 2001. It has been subject to a number of revisions. The current conceptual framework project is being conducted in phases and the present version, issued in September 2010, contains two completed chapters, namely Chapters 1 and 3 (see below). Chapter 2, which remains to be added, will deal with the concept of the reporting entity, while Chapter 4 contains the remainder of the framework document issued in 1989. There are two further sections at the end of the document which discuss the rationale underlying the treatment of items included in Chapters 1 and 3, and a table on the final page which shows how the contents of the 1989 and 2010 documents correspond. The 2010 IASB Framework document deals with:

(a) the objective of general purpose financial reporting (Chapter 1)

(b) the qualitative characteristics of useful financial information (Chapter 3)

(c) the definition, recognition and measurement of the elements from which financial statements are constructed (Chapter 4)

(d) concepts of capital and capital maintenance (Chapter 4).

Items (a) to (d) will now be considered.

4.2.2   The objective of general purpose financial reporting

> The objective of general purpose financial reporting is to provide financial information about the reporting entity that is useful to existing and potential investors and other creditors in making decisions about providing resources to the entity. Those decisions involve buying, selling, or holding equity and debt instruments, and providing or settling loans and other forms of credit.
>
> IASB Framework, paragraph OB2

The IASB Framework quite clearly specifies the primary parties for whom/which general financial reports are intended. Although it acknowledges that there will be other interested parties for whom/which such financial reports will be useful, they are not the main intended target groups. For the interests of user groups such as existing and potential investors and other creditors, see Section 2.4.

The IASB Framework states that other aspects of the conceptual framework flow from the above objective, namely a reporting entity concept, the qualitative characteristics of, and the constraint on, useful financial information, elements of financial statements, recognition, measurement, presentation and disclosure.

The IASB Framework stresses the inherent need for useful information about an entity's economic resources and claims against the entity, and the effects of transactions and other events that change the entity's resources and claims.

4.2.3   Qualitative characteristics of useful financial information

Chapter 3 of the IASB Framework identifies and discusses the qualitative characteristics of information that are likely to be most useful to existing and potential investors, lenders and other creditors, subject to the pervasive constraint of the cost of providing such information.

> If financial information is to be useful, it must be relevant and faithfully represent what it purports to represent. The usefulness of financial information is enhanced if it is comparable, verifiable, timely and understandable.
>
> IASB Framework, paragraph QC4

Relevance and faithful representation are deemed to be fundamental qualitative characteristics. Comparability, verifiability, timeliness and understandability are deemed to be enhancing qualitative characteristics, that is, they enhance the usefulness of information that is relevant and faithfully represented. These different characteristics are discussed below.

4.2.4   Fundamental qualitative characteristics

Relevance

Financial information is deemed to be relevant if it helps users make decisions. This means it should help them assess past, present or likely future events. It may help users to make a decision, confirm what they had thought might happen and/or correct an inaccurate evaluation. Therefore, financial information is often said to be predictive or confirmatory, though the two ideas are related. However, as mentioned previously in Sections 3.7 and 4.2.2, financial statements are prepared primarily for owners and/or shareholders and creditors, so the immediate needs of other users are unlikely to be specifically addressed. If other users were to be considered, then it would mean preparing financial statements for each individual user, which would take considerable time.

The IASB considered the issue of whether there should be identified groups of users and decided in favour of this, because the IASB Framework would have otherwise been too vague. A common criticism of financial statements is that they are often published too late (and are thus too outdated) to enable effective decision making. Considering explicitly the needs of other users by preparing separate financial statements would compound this problem, especially as some users' needs might conflict with others'. On this basis too, the IASB rejected the idea that there should be a defined 'hierarchy' of users. Information, then, needs to be both relevant and provided in an acceptable time frame.

The relevance of information may be affected by materiality. Information may be considered material if its omission from, or misstatement in, financial statements would affect or distort the economic decisions of users. A lender, for instance, might choose not to make a loan to a company if it considered that the assets offered as security for the loan were incorrectly valued. If information would not make a difference, then it is regarded as immaterial. Information that is immaterial can be understandable, relevant, verifiable and comparable, etc., but if it does not make a difference in any way, these other characteristics do not matter and would be ignored. There are different ways of quantitatively measuring or assessing materiality, such as by reference to a certain percentage of profit (before tax is deducted). Materiality is of great importance to auditors and whether an omission or misstatement is material or not will depend on its size in a particular context. It thus provides a cut-off point in terms of overall usefulness.

Relevance can also be affected by the nature of information, which in certain cases alone determines relevance (e.g., a legal requirement to disclose information). If information is required by law, as in the case of disclosing company directors' emoluments (i.e., the salaries and other benefits they receive), it will be material whatever the size or value of items involved as the legal requirement will make it so.

Faithful representation
This means that relevant economic phenomena should be represented in words and numbers in a way that is as complete, neutral and free from error as possible. 'Complete' means that all information should be included which is necessary for the user to understand the phenomena being represented. 'Neutral' means that the representation should be without any bias, that is, it has not been manipulated in any way to increase the likelihood that users will receive it favourably or unfavourably. 'Free from error' does not necessarily mean accuracy in all respects, but it means that there

should be no omissions or errors in the numerical or verbal representation of phenomena and that the process used to produce the representation should be selected and applied without error. For example, if a company were preparing its financial statements just before it was due to go to court for a case against it to be heard (e.g., for an allegedly faulty product, which had injured its purchaser), it might not know whether it would win or lose the case, which would make the financial effect very difficult to gauge, and cause great uncertainty as to what the company should include in its financial statements. The company could only represent the financial effect in numbers and/or words in accordance with the best legal opinion available.

The IASB Framework suggests that:

> The most efficient and effective process for applying the fundamental qualitative characteristics would usually be as follows (subject to the effects of enhancing characteristics and the cost constraint ...). First, identify an economic phenomenon that has the potential to be useful to users of the entity's financial information. Second, identify the type of information about that phenomenon that would be most relevant if it is available and can be faithfully represented. Third, determine whether that information is available and can be represented. If so, the process of satisfying the fundamental qualitative characteristic ends at that point. If not, the process is repeated with the next most relevant type of information.
>
> IASB Framework, paragraph QC18

4.2.5   Enhancing qualitative characteristics

Comparability

Comparability means that financial statements should be comparable with the financial statements of other, like entities and with the financial statements of the same entity for earlier accounting periods. In this context, 'entity' usually means a company of some kind, as the financial statements of other organisations (e.g., sole traders and partnerships) are often not readily available for comparison purposes. Key elements of comparability are disclosing how any transaction/event is accounted for, which is referred to as an accounting policy, and applying accounting policies consistently (treating and disclosing like items in the same way, and in the same way from one accounting period to another). Consistency helps achieve comparability. However, a company should not apply the same accounting policies blindly from year to year, but should keep them under review and change them if more relevant or reliable policies are available. Companies are required to disclose their accounting policies, which helps users make allowance for the effect of different policies on company financial statements. If a company changes its accounting policies, this must be disclosed, together with the effect of the change.

Verifiability

This means that users can be assured that information faithfully represents the economic phenomena it claims to represent.

Information may be verified directly, for example, by observation, as in counting cash or inventory. It may also be verified indirectly by 'checking inputs to a model, formula or other technique and recalculating the outputs by using the same methodology' (IASB Framework, paragraph QC27).

Timeliness

This means that information should be available to users in time to help influence their decisions. Older information is generally less useful, unless one specifically needs this kind of material (e.g., to identify and evaluate trends).

Understandability

Inevitably some understanding of business and accounting is required to enable users to understand financial statements, and the extent to which they do so will be a combination of their knowledge and abilities. However, users are assumed to have a 'reasonable knowledge of business and economic activities' and to 'review and analyse information diligently' (IASB Framework, paragraph QC32), although even knowledgeable and diligent users may require the help of an appropriately qualified adviser to understand some of the complexities inherent in financial information. Companies do differ in the amount of effort they put into analysing, aggregating and classifying financial information to make it user-friendly, but information should not be excluded simply because it may be too complex for certain users to understand.

The IASB Framework suggests that while enhancing qualitative characteristics should be used to the maximum extent possible, there can be no prescribed order in which to apply them, as circumstances will dictate what is required. However, nothing can make information useful that is irrelevant or not represented faithfully in the first place.

Constraints and limitations

From the above discussion, it is evident that some characteristics militate against others. Information that is more relevant may be less verifiable, while the opposite may also be true. Timing and timeliness are also important in terms of verifiability. It may be a case of making the best possible compromise between timeliness and verifiability. Furthermore, the benefits and costs of providing information need to be considered. Unless there is a legal requirement to provide information, there is always a trade-off between the benefits and costs: the latter should not exceed the former. The IASB Framework only considers the cost constraint.

Financial statements are required to show a 'true and fair view' of or 'present fairly' (the precise words used are jurisdiction-specific) the financial position, performance and changes in financial position of an entity. It is an auditor's job to report on this, and this will be considered further in Unit 6.

4.2.6 The definition, recognition and measurement of the elements from which financial statements are constructed

Chapter 4 of the IASB Framework contains material about the definition, recognition and measurement of the elements from which financial statements are constructed and concepts of capital and capital maintenance, which have not, at the time of writing, been updated from the 1989 document. This material is expected to be updated in future.

Chapter 4 begins with a brief discussion of one of the underlying assumptions on which financial statements should be prepared, namely the going concern basis. The other main assumption on which financial statements should be prepared is the accruals basis, but this is not actually mentioned in Chapter 4. The accruals basis is briefly referred to in Chapter 1, but it does not give very much detail (it is almost taken for granted). However, as this concept is so important, it is explained in more detail below.

The accruals basis

Under this basis:

> Accrual accounting depicts the effects of transactions and other events and circumstances on a reporting entity's economic resources and claims in the periods in which those effects occur, even if the resulting cash receipts and payments occur in a different period.
>
> IASB Framework, paragraph OB17

This is similar to what used to be referred to as the accruals or matching concept where expenditure should be charged to the period that has benefited from a cost or expense incurred. This meant that all revenue or other benefit received should be matched to the expenditure incurred in generating that revenue or benefit. Where expenditure has been incurred during a period for which revenue or benefit has not yet been received, the expenditure should be omitted from the calculation of profit for that period and accrued until the period when the revenue or benefit results (e.g., annual buildings insurance paid mid-accounting period which is valid for the first six months of the next period).

This also applies in reverse when it is the benefit that is received before expenditure occurs (e.g., electricity consumed before a period end not yet charged for, as the billing date for electricity is after the period end).

The going concern basis

This means that when preparing financial statements, values are based on the assumption that the business will continue into the foreseeable future without the intention or need 'to liquidate or curtail materially the scale of its operations' (IASB Framework, paragraph 4.1). If such an intention exists, it means that the financial statements may have to be prepared on a different basis and, if so, that basis will need to be disclosed.

Activity 4.1

Jones Ltd has prepared its financial statements for many years on a going concern basis, stating assets at their cost, less a deduction for an amount representing how much they have been worn away by use (this is referred to as the **historical cost method**, and you will learn more about it below and also in Unit 3). However, owing to a sudden downturn in the market for its goods, the company thinks it can only continue trading for another six to eight months at most. Imagine that you are about to prepare the financial statements for Jones Ltd. What do you think you should do now that you are aware that it is unlikely to continue to operate for the foreseeable future?

Spend a few minutes writing down what you would do.

Feedback

Instead of valuing all the assets based on their historical cost, you would need to value them on the basis of what they could be sold for if the business stopped operating. This is often referred to as a **break-up basis**.

Activity 4.2

What valuation-related problems do you think a business cessation might create for an accountant?

Spend a few minutes writing down a list of the problems you can think of.

Feedback

A choice would need to be made about whether it is likely the business could be sold intact to someone who would then continue to use all the assets to do what they are currently doing. The individual assets would probably have a higher value if this is possible. Buyers might not want, for example, specialised inventory or a 20 year old machine, say, unless it was going to be used to do what it has always done, nor would they want a custom-designed factory unless they were going to produce similar products within it.

As a general rule when checking whether the going concern assumption should hold, it should not hold if:

1   the business is going to close down in the near future

2   a shortage of cash makes it almost certain that the business will have to cease trading

3   a large part of the business will almost certainly have to be closed down because of a shortage of cash.

Definition of elements

In paragraph 4.2, the IASB Framework says that the financial effects of transactions and other events should be grouped into broad classes and portrayed in financial statements according to their economic characteristics. These broad classes form the elements from which the financial statements are constructed. The balance sheet elements are assets, liability and equity. The income statement elements are income and expenses. Elements will usually be analysed into sub-groups. For example, assets and liabilities may be classified by their nature or function. Paragraph 4.4 of the IASB Framework defines the elements as follows.

(a)   An *asset* is a resource controlled by the entity as a result of past events and from which future economic benefits are expected to flow to the entity.

(b)   A *liability* is a present obligation of the entity arising from past events, the settlement of which is expected to result in an outflow from the entity of resources embodying economic benefits.

(c) *Equity* is the residual interest in the assets of the entity after deducting all its liabilities.

The elements of income and expenses are defined as follows (paragraph 4.25):

(a) *Income* is increases in economic benefits during the accounting period in the form of inflows or enhancements of assets or decreases of liabilities that result in increases in equity, other than those relating to contributions from equity participants.

(b) *Expenses* are decreases in economic benefits during the accounting period in the form of outflows or depletions of assets or incurrences of liabilities that result in decreases in equity, other than those relating to distributions to equity participants.

Recognition of elements

Recognition means the process of incorporating into the balance sheet or income statement items which meet the definition of an element (as given above) and have a cost or value that can be measured reliably. For example, something would be incorporated into the balance sheet as an asset when it is probable that future economic benefits will flow to the entity from it and it has a cost or value that can be measured reliably.

Measurement of elements

Measurement means the process of determining the monetary amount at which the elements of the financial statements are to be included in the balance sheet and income statement. This involves the selection of a particular basis of measurement. Paragraph 4.55 of the IASB Framework includes the following bases of measurement.

(a) *Historical cost.* Assets are recorded at the amount of cash or cash equivalents paid or the fair value of the consideration given to acquire them at the time of their acquisition. Liabilities are recorded at the amount of proceeds received in exchange for the obligation, or in some circumstances (e.g., taxes), at the amounts of cash or cash equivalents expected to be paid to satisfy the liability in the normal course of business.

(b) *Current cost.* Assets are carried at the amount of cash or cash equivalents that would have to be paid if the same or an equivalent asset was acquired currently. Liabilities are carried at the undiscounted amount of cash or cash equivalents that would be required to settle the obligation currently.

(c) *Realisable (settlement) value.* Assets are carried at the amount of cash or cash equivalents that could currently be obtained by selling the asset in an orderly disposal. Liabilities are carried at their settlement values, that is, the undiscounted amounts of cash or cash equivalents expected to be paid to satisfy the liabilities in the normal course of business.

(d) *Present value.* Assets are carried at the present discounted value of the future net cash inflows that the item is expected to generate in the normal course of business. Liabilities are carried at the present discounted value of the future net cash outflows that are expected to be required to settle the liabilities in the normal course of business. (You will learn more about discounted values in B292.)

The IASB Framework goes on to comment that the measurement basis most commonly adopted is historical cost, but that this is usually combined with other measurement bases. For example, inventories are usually carried at the lower of cost and net realisable value (see Unit 3), whereas marketable securities may be carried at market value and pension liabilities are carried at their present value. The current cost basis has been frequently used as a response to the inability of the historical cost accounting model to deal with the effects of changing prices of non-monetary assets.

4.2.7 Concepts of capital and capital maintenance

You will remember from Section 1.4.2 that there are different ways of showing a financial position (balance sheet), either in a horizontal or vertical format, and that capital may be regarded as a particular kind of liability. It is the amount invested by the owner, against which the owner may make drawings and which would be repayable in full to the owner as and if the business permanently ceased operations. As shown in Figures 3 and 4 (in Section 1.4.2), any profit generated by business operations is added in to capital and increases the overall value of the half of the balance sheet in which it is included. (You will find out how this all works, when you learn in detail about double-entry bookkeeping in Units 2 and 3.) In the vertical balance sheet format, you will see that the top half shows assets less liabilities, and the bottom half shows capital plus profits, and the two halves add up to the same figure. This figure is referred to as net assets or net worth. This is a measure of the wealth or 'well-offness' of the business. The concept of capital maintenance is concerned with how a business defines the capital/wealth (investment in the business) which it wishes to maintain. Put simply, a business has maintained its capital if it has at least as much capital at the end of an accounting period as it had at the beginning.

The IASB Framework (paragraph 4.59) suggests that there are two basic concepts of capital:

- The *financial concept of capital*. This refers to invested money or invested purchasing power, hence giving rise to the further concept of financial (or money) capital maintenance. Under this concept, capital means net assets or equity.

- The *physical concept of capital*. This refers to the productive capability of a business – thus giving rise to the further concept of physical capital maintenance.

These concepts are discussed further below.

If a business has a net worth according to its financial statements of £100,000 on 1 January 20X9, it must also have a value in its financial statements of £100,000 at 31 December 20X9, to be as well off at the end of the period. Take the example of Mr Jones, a sole trader who has introduced no new capital and has not withdrawn any (via drawings). If he started with a value according to his financial group and other users (e.g., disclosure about a significant reduction in company activities).

Chapter 1 does not set out the underlying principles for financial statement preparation (such as the accruals and going concern basis given by the IASB Framework), but it does go on to suggest that information is required in the four areas of financial performance, financial position, generation and use of cash, and financial adaptability. These areas are discussed below.

Financial performance

This comprises the return obtained from the resources a business controls, and is available from the income statement (profit). It facilitates evaluation of past (and anticipated) management performance and management stewardship, assessment of capacity to generate cash, how effectively resources have been utilised and enables users to modify their expectations. An emphasis on 'stewardship' here ties in with the focus on the investor group as the primary user group, which aligns with the focus adopted by the IASB Framework.

Financial position

This is usually provided by an examination of the balance sheet to show a business's assets and liabilities, sources of finance, liquidity and solvency, and ability to adapt to changes.

Generation and use of cash

Such information will be available from a cash flow statement, which shows cash flows in and out of a business as a result of its operating, investment and financing activities.

Financial adaptability

This refers to a business's ability to alter the amount and timing of its cash flows so that it can respond to unexpected needs or opportunities, such as raising or repaying finance, disposing of assets and changing the cash flows from operations.

Chapter 2: The reporting entity

Chapter 2 focuses on identifying when an entity should report (e.g., when there is a legitimate demand for information and there is a cohesive economic unit) and the type of activities to include (e.g., activities under the unit's direct control and, in defined cases, indirect control). The chapter devotes considerable effort to defining terms, such as 'control'.

The IASB Framework originally did not contain a section on the reporting entity, but the version issued in September 2010 indicated plans to include a chapter on this in due course.

Chapter 3: The qualitative characteristics of financial information

The ASB Statement contains the same general qualitative characteristics of information as the IASB Framework (see Sections 4.2.2 and 4.2.3). However, slightly different focus and emphasis is laid on certain aspects, as is shown in Figure 10.

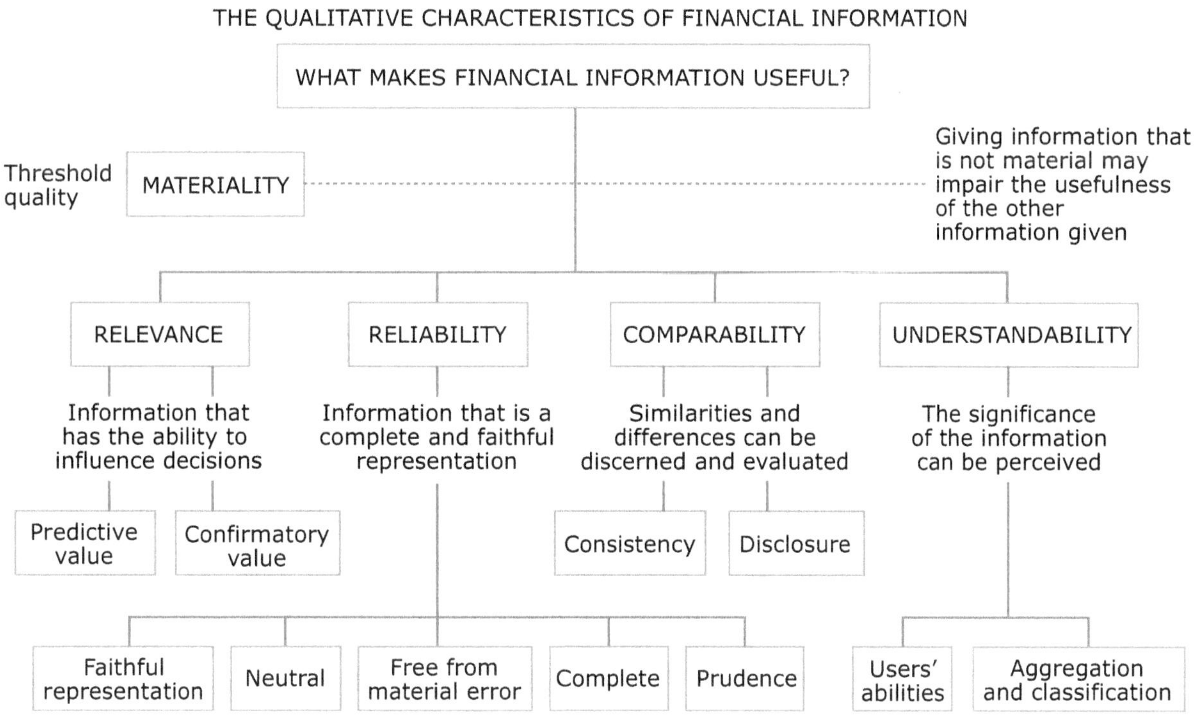

THE QUALITATIVE CHARACTERISTICS OF FINANCIAL INFORMATION

Figure 10 What makes information useful

The concept of prudence included in Figure 10 means that caution must be used when preparing financial statements, and in estimating the outcome of uncertain events. However, it does not mean that the most pessimistic interpretation should automatically be adopted. A balance needs to be struck so that assets, income and gains are not overstated and liabilities, expenses and losses are not understated. Equally the exercise of prudence does not permit the deliberate understatement of assets, etc., nor the overstatement of liabilities, etc.

The ASB does not discuss verifiability or timeliness specifically, as the IASB Framework does, although (arguably) they could perceivably be covered by reliability and relevance. Neither the ASB nor the IASB now discusses the issue of '**substance over form**' (i.e., reflecting the economic nature of an event, transaction, etc., as opposed to its precise legal form).

The ASB Statement also includes an extensive discussion of how the different characteristics may militate against one another and of the possible trade-offs between them. The ASB treats the concept of a 'true and fair view' as an underlying concept at the foundation of the Statement, and discusses it not in the main chapters of the Statement, but much more prominently in a separate introduction to the Statement.

Chapter 4: The elements of financial statements

These are the same as in the IASB Framework, though in addition the ASB uses the terms 'ownership interest', 'gains' and 'losses' as equivalent to 'equity', 'income' and 'expenses' in the IASB Framework. The ASB Statement also includes and defines:

- contributions by the owners as increases in ownership interest resulting from transfers from owners in their capacity as owners
- distributions to the owners as decreases in ownership interest resulting from transfers to owners in their capacity as owners.

The IASB Framework treats the above two items as movements within equity.

presentation issues. Rather than being dealt with in the relevant chapters and therefore in isolation from each other, they are dealt with together in this chapter'.

Chapter 8, therefore, deals with the way that results of entities are combined. This topic is not included in B291, so Session 4 will not discuss this further.

4.4 Other conceptual frameworks

The ASB Statement is one of several national conceptual frameworks. Documents produced by leading accounting standard setters, such as those in Australia, Canada, New Zealand and the USA, all utilise similar principles and explanations, though there are differences between them – some more significant than others. The US Financial Accounting Standards Board (FASB) pronouncements (a series of 'Concepts Statements') have been of particular importance in a worldwide context, given the USA's dominance in the global economy. However, the US approach is much more rules-based than that of other countries (other than, perhaps, continental Europe), which tend to be more principles-based. This has proven to be something of a stumbling block in moves towards developing a global convergence of accounting standards. However, the IASB and FASB are presently working on a 'Conceptual Framework Convergence Project', which may result in changes to the current FASB and IASB frameworks. The new exposure draft of the *Conceptual Framework for Financial Reporting: the Reporting Entity* (as mentioned in Section 4.3.1) is actually a result of this convergence project, as it is a document issued jointly by the IASB and FASB.

Summary

In Session 4, you have learned about the IASB Framework as a development to meet the need for an underlying theoretical basis for accounting and financial reporting, and about the ASB Statement of Principles as the UK's attempt to implement that Framework. You have learned about the differences and similarities between these two documents in terms of defining and understanding the qualitative characteristics of financial reporting information; defining, understanding and applying accounting principles, concepts and conventions; understanding and explaining different concepts of profit measurement and recognition; and identifying and explaining the main characteristics of alternative valuation bases for assets and liabilities. You will appreciate how differences in applications of concepts and principles can produce different calculations, treatments and presentations of the figures which can appear in a set of financial statements.

Unit summary

You have now come to the end of Unit 1, the first unit of B291 *Financial accounting*.

This unit has acted as an overall introduction to the module, by identifying a number of concepts and ideas, which will be explored and developed in greater depth in subsequent units. When you encounter these again, you will be aware that you need to get to grips with them as fundamental topics, as, for example, in the case of double-entry bookkeeping, which immediately follows in Units 2–4. Therefore, Unit 1 acts as an essential foundation for developing the specific subject matter addressed in subsequent units. Do not be afraid to refer back to Unit 1 when you encounter material in more depth in later units as it will help remind you of what you have learned already.

In conjunction with all this, each session in Unit 1 introduced a number of subjects which are important in their own right.

Session 1 introduced the main purposes and objectives of bookkeeping and accounting.

Session 2 taught you about the context in which accounting fulfils its various functions, especially in terms of organisations of different kinds and the needs of various users of accounting information.

Session 3 examined the main environmental influences and constraints on business, accounting and accountants and introduced you to regulatory frameworks.

Session 4 considered the theoretical frameworks for accounting and financial reporting, and their underlying concepts and principles, and the qualitative characteristics of accounting information.

Before you move on to Unit 2, the following self-assessed questions provide you with the opportunity to check whether you have understood the material in this unit.

Self-assessed Questions

Please note that in the suggested answers that follow each of these self-assessed questions (SAQs), the answers are only given briefly in outline form, with a cross reference to the section of the main text where relevant material is provided. These self-assessed questions are representative of the type of questions that could be set in the end of course unseen examination. Full written answers are not provided, as writing styles, how people include content and discuss it, etc., can be different from individual to individual, and answers which may look very different can each be good, original, and even creative. There are several ways, for example, of writing an effective answer to address the 'critically discuss' requirement as in the SAQs here. This does not mean 'describe' or 'give a list': it means evaluating or assessing the merits or demerits of a particular set of facts, lines of reasoning, etc., to arrive at a reasoned conclusion. This requires practice and no two people will do it in the same way! You will need to develop your own style of producing written answers. Remember too that written answers need a proper introduction, and should be as full as the time allowed permits and should be written in good English with proper use of grammar, syntax and punctuation.

Acknowledgements

Grateful acknowledgement is made to the following sources:

Text

Activity 2.3: Annual Report (2010) www.j-sainsbury.co.uk. Material made available courtesy of J Sainsbury plc

Figures

Figure 7a: FRC Ltd Board 2009. © Financial Reporting Council 2009

Figure 7b: Financial Reporting Council (2012) 'FRC structure and regulatory procedures', www.frc.org.uk

Figure 8: IFRS Foundation (2012) 'How we are structured', www.ifrs.org

Figure 9: © IASB 2009

Figure 10: Accounting Standards Board (1999) Statement of Principles for Financial Reporting. ASB

Illustrations

Page 8: Portrait of Luca Pacioli (c. 1445–c.1514). © The Bridgeman Art Library

Page 44: John Morris, www.CartoonStock.com

Page 45: © David Brown, www.CartoonStock.com

Page 45: Ms Lat 209 fol.6v Jupiter, detail of fruit and grain merchants, from 'De Sphaera', c.1470 (vellum) (detail of 308309), De Predis, Cristoforo (1440/45–86) (attributed to) / Biblioteca Estense, Modena, Italy / Giraudon / The Bridgeman Art Library

Page 49: Neil Bennet, www.CartoonStock.com

Page 50: Copyright 2002 by Randy Glasbergen. www.glasbergen.com

Page 61: With permission from Bill Monroe, www.MonroeArtist.com

Page 62: With permission from Bill Monroe, www.MonroeArtist.com

Every effort has been made to contact copyright holders. If any have been inadvertently overlooked the publishers will be pleased to make the necessary arrangements at the first opportunity.

-